The Catskill
PARK

The Catskill PARK

INSIDE THE BLUE LINE

The Forest Preserve & Mountain Communities
of America's First Wilderness

Norman J. Van Valkenburgh
and
Christopher W. Olney

Principal photography by Thomas Teich

BLACK·DOME

Published by

Black Dome Press Corp.
1011 Route 296
Hensonville, New York 12439
www.blackdomepress.com
Tel: (518) 734-6357

First Edition Paperback 2004
Copyright © 2004 Christopher W. Olney, Norman J. Van Valkenburgh

Library of Congress Cataloging-in-Publication Data

Van Valkenburgh, Norman J. (Norman James), 1930–
    The Catskill Park: inside the blue line, the forest preserve & mountain communities of America's
    first wilderness / by Norman J. Van Valkenburgh and Christopher W. Olney; principal photography by
    Thomas Teich.— 1st ed. pbk.
        p. cm.
    Includes index.

    ISBN 1-883789-42-7

1. Catskill Forest Preserve (N.Y.)--History. 2. Catskill Forest Preserve (N.Y.)—History—Pictorial works.
I. Olney, Christopher W. II. Teich, Thomas. III. Title.

F127.C3V37 2004
974.7'38—dc22
                                            2004021635

Cover photographs by Thomas Teich. For details see photography section beginning page 95.
Design: Ron Toelke Associates
Printed in the USA

Photograph by Chris Olney

*"In the beginning,
all the world was America."*

John Locke

DEDICATION

This book is being published on the occasion of the one hundredth anniversary of the Catskill Park, which was created by the New York State Legislature on April 5, 1904.

Much of the history of the Catskill Park and forest preserve has appeared in booklets and articles previously written by Norman J. Van Valkenburgh, but this material has not been easily accessible to a public audience. That historical information is presented here again and brought up to date. Perhaps just as important as the presentation of the history of the Catskill Park and forest preserve, however, is the authors' intention to offer some thoughts and perspective on the uniqueness and importance of our great state's second-largest park, and perhaps spark renewed interest in, and appreciation and awareness of, this great resource in our backyards.

Many refer to the Catskill Mountains as "America's First Wilderness" because its location upstream of old New Amsterdam put it in the path of the first Europeans settling the Hudson Valley during the 1600s. As novelist Wallace Stegner so eloquently stated, "Wilderness was the challenge against which our character as a people was formed," and this was as true for the Catskills as it was for any place in North America. The wilderness areas that we enjoy in the Catskills today are indeed a reminder of the challenges and opportunities that faced those who ventured into these untamed blue mountains long before us. There are many reasons why the Catskill Park and forest preserve are special and unique; however, they are often overlooked by people who go elsewhere in the Northeast for their solace and recreation, and also by many of the local residents and second-home owners who have only a vague awareness of the wilderness in their backyard. The Catskill Park is often overshadowed by the attention paid to the Adirondacks given the sheer size of the Adirondack Park (which is the largest park in the contiguous United States). The Catskill Park is also often overshadowed by the attention given to that other great landscape feature of the Catskill Mountains—the New York City Watershed. The huge quantity and excellent quality of unfiltered, potable water supplied to that vast metropolis on a daily basis certainly owes much to the large tracts of "forever wild" land in the New York City Watershed that is the Catskill state forest preserve. But there are other very important reasons why we should continue to cherish and protect this great asset that was bestowed on us by forward-thinking and forward-acting individuals. This is true not just for the state land we know as the forest preserve, but also for the larger Catskill Park and the people and communities it contains.

And so it is that this book is dedicated to those individuals who had, and continue to have, the foresight to create, perpetuate, and be responsible stewards of the Catskill Park and the public and private lands within it for the enjoyment and benefit of the people of New York. 🍃

CONTENTS

Foreword   10
Professor Michael Kudish

Acknowledgments   13

The Catskill Park in Perspective   15
Christopher W. Olney

History of the Catskill Park and Forest Preserve   27
Norman J. Van Valkenburgh

Land Management   89
Christopher W. Olney

A Catskill Park Portfolio   95
Catskills Photography

The Future of the Catskill Park   141
Christopher W. Olney

Appendix A   149
Charles Carpenter 1886 Report to the
State Forest Commission on the Catskill Preserve

Appendix B   202
Catskill Park Metes-and-Bounds Description

Index   204

About the authors   207

FOREWORD

Norman J. Van Valkenburgh is one of Edward G. West's disciples. For those who knew Ed West, former superintendent of land acquisition for the State of New York, there is no need here to describe his unparalleled knowledge of the historical surveys of the Catskills, Adirondacks, and other portions of New York State. Norm succeeded Ed when Ed retired, maintaining the same high level of historical survey knowledge. I have used Norm's books and articles many times as reference material for my own writing; he provides historical detail on state lands, e.g. acquisition, campgrounds, lean-tos, trails, wilderness areas, wild forests, intensive use areas, fish hatcheries, etc.—extant and abandoned—unavailable anywhere else. If it weren't for Norm's writings, all this detail would be inaccessible to the public, buried in the New York State Department of Environmental Conservation's archives, or even worse, discarded.

I first met Christopher W. Olney in 1999 at The Catskill Center where he had recently begun the work of its director of conservation; we had so much in common that it seemed that we had been friends for years. Chris is a superb geographer and cartographer, among his many other skills. To be able to combine excerpts from Norm's writings and weave them together with those of other writers and his own prose into a well-structured, factually accurate manuscript is far beyond the ability of most authors. I wondered why he had so little time this year to join me in the field for further explorations of Catskill bogs; now I know why.

When the editor of Black Dome Press requested that I write a foreword, he asked for a view of the Catskills from a historian trained in the biological sciences. This writer has been studying the Catskills' forest for over forty years in an attempt to reconstruct its development from the end of the ice age to the present. Like Norm Van Valkenburgh, this writer also was most fortunate to accompany and learn from Ed West in the field. Vegetational History of the Catskill High Peaks, a 1971 dissertation, was my first compilation of detail, while the book, The Catskill Forest: History, published in 2000, was the second. Studies of the forest continue, with a concentration at present on identification and radiocarbon-dating of plant fossils preserved in peat bogs for up to twelve thousand years.

The views of this forest historian are often different from those of the two authors and many other writers. My views, ideally objective, are almost as if they originate from the forest itself, outside the world of human activity. These views are also from a perspective of over several millennia, going back to a time when an absence of people prevailed.

What would the domain of the Catskill Park be like today if the park had not been created?

To find out, all we need to do is hike to one or more of three ranges of mountains: (1) from Bearpen via Grand Gorge to Utsayantha, (2) from Mount Pisgah (Delaware County) via Plattekill Mountain to the Moresville Range in Delaware County, and (3) from Mount Pisgah (Greene County; yes, there are two peaks with the same name) to Huntersfield Mountain. These ranges are in the Catskills because the ridgelines are at such high elevations, much above 3000 feet, but they all lie outside the Catskill Park. If there were no Catskill Park, almost the whole Catskill region would presently look like this:

Pastures climb higher on the slopes of these three ranges, in some cases as high as 3000 feet, the result of a complete removal of the forest.

There is no forest preserve here outside the park. Much of the Huntersfield Range is covered by state forest plantations, which are harvested.

Forestry practices are all but chaotic on private lands on these three ranges. Many different landowners and their logging contractors practice very different kinds of silvicultural methods, or none at all, in close proximity to one another. A plethora of duplicating skid roads climbs up from the valleys to the ridgelines at frequent intervals, usually one per landowner.

Some tracts of forest land that have remained in the same family for many genera-

tions have very consistent, multiple-use, long-range management plans based on sound scientific forestry principles, such as those recommended by the Catskill Forest Association. Unfortunately, the majority of tracts have owners with no such management plan, and all kinds of problems result, such as soil erosion from steep skid roads, and huge, impenetrable, nearly permanent blackberry patches that greatly inhibit natural tree regeneration.

There are also power lines, communication towers, snowmobile and all-terrain vehicle trails, and hunting camp buildings nearly everywhere. In regions adjacent to the Catskills, such as the Hudson and Mohawk valleys, the Southern Tier, and the Finger Lakes, we expect to see such intense human activity. But in the higher-elevation Catskills we may not. These three ranges little resemble the portion of the Catskills within the park.

As a result, first-growth forest is very rare in these three ranges, occurring in a few isolated small pockets.

In contrast, the forest preserve is controlled by a single plan for the whole region, and for the Adirondacks, by a single landowner—the people of New York State—and managed by the Department of Environmental Conservation.

What is the likely future of the forests in the forest preserve, given their "forever wild" status?

One must look at the climax forests, pioneer forests, and escarpment oak forests, each separately, to make predictions. The following predictions should work well provided we have no forest threats created by organisms introduced from other parts of the world.

Climax forests of northern hardwoods (sugar maple, red maple, beech, yellow birch, black cherry), with or without associated conifers (red spruce, balsam fir, and/or eastern hemlock), should remain the same for centuries more as they have for the last 7,000 or 8,000 years. Natural disturbances on a local level come and go—wind, snow, ice, drought, flood, and native defoliators. This is all normal in climax forests consisting of shade-tolerant species that readily perpetuate themselves.

Pioneer forests, which had been cleared for pasture or charcoal, or burned only once, should revert back to their original, pre-disturbance state: the climax forest. This will require between 100 and 200 years. Current pioneer species such as paper birch, eastern white pine, red cherry, aspens, eastern red cedar, and hawthorns will all but disappear because of their lack of shade tolerance.

Forests along the Catskills' escarpment and in the lower Esopus Basin, burned over for millennia and now dominated by oaks, hickories, pitch pine, mountain laurel, and blueberries, should be replaced by northern hardwoods climax forests. This will also require between 100 to 200 years and will depend on the seed source availability of the northern hardwoods.

But conditions in reality are not so ideal and simple. The above predictions may prove inaccurate because of a recent acceleration, at an alarming rate, of the introduction of foreign organisms that threaten the forest. When this writer was preparing his dissertation in 1971, all that forest ecologists worried about were gypsy moth, chestnut blight, and Dutch elm disease. In the last quarter century or so, however, we have come to fear beech bark disease (present for nearly a century, but a serious problem only recently), hemlock wooly adelgid, pear thrips on sugar maple, and fungus disease problems on butternut, sycamore, flowering dogwood, and white ash. All this is exacerbated by acid precipitation, which can decrease the general vigor of the forest. The Department of Environmental Conservation and the interested public must unite and create an army of people to control and stifle these threats, and prevent additional ones from attacking; if we do not, we will see a drastic altering of the nature of our forests in unpredictable ways unheard of in the past.

What is the value of the Catskill Park from the forest historian's perspective?

The Catskill Park, making possible the forest preserve within it, provides a great opportunity for ecologists and other scientists to examine forests with little or no human disturbance. These forests act like controls in laboratory experiments, where no treatment is performed. Undisturbed forests, though very complex, are still simpler than ones heavily disturbed by people. If we can best understand first how the undisturbed forest "works," we can then much better understand how to manage forests that have and will experience varying degrees of human activity.

Michael Kudish, Ph.D., Professor
Division of Forestry, Paul Smith's College
August 8, 2004

ACKNOWLEDGMENTS

There is no shortage of people who recognized the merits of this book project from the onset and who gave freely of their support and assistance in bringing it to fruition. Chief among these is Debbie Allen at Black Dome Press, who really knows the publishing business well and is a master at organizing all of the critical elements of creating a book in a timely fashion.

The idea for this book was born in the early meetings of the Catskill Park Centennial Planning Committee, which was ably and tirelessly chaired by Helen Chase, board member of The Catskill Center for Conservation and Development. As we moved through to publication, Helen continued to offer her valuable assistance. The entire Catskill Park Centennial Planning Committee is to be congratulated on their hard work and accomplishments in bringing forth many events, announcements, and lasting contributions to commemorate the Catskill Park. The committee consisted of staff of the New York State Department of Environmental Conservation (NYSDEC), members of regional outdoor and conservation organizations, artists, writers, performers, historians, educators, and interested individuals.

Color images for this book would not have been possible were it not for the generous financial assistance of The Catskill Center and its executive director, Tom Alworth, and the Friends of the Catskill Interpretive Center and its principle directors, Jim Infante and Sherret Chase Sr. These two organizations and their directors recognized the value of this book in increasing the public's awareness and appreciation of the Catskill Park and wanted to make the book a centerpiece of the 2004 Catskill Park Centennial celebration. The grant from The Catskill Center came from funds earmarked for the Catskill Park Anniversary activities by New York State Senator John Bonacic, and the grant from the Friends of the Catskill Interpretive Center came from funds provided by the Wallace Genetic Foundation for activities related to the advancement of the public's knowledge of the Catskill Park.

Others who supported this project early on include: Jack McShane, whose personal support and encouragement is much appreciated; John Keating and Jim Jensen at the New York State Department of Environmental Conservation's Bureau of Real Property, who helped us access state land acquisition files at NYSDEC headquarters in Albany; NYSDEC Region 3 Natural Resources Supervisor Bill Rudge and Regional Foresters Jeff Rider and Frank Parks, who clarified certain forest preserve information; Paul Grondahl, who provided certain historic information; Dr. Michael Kudish, who graciously contributed the foreword and who has done so much to educate us about the forests of the Catskills; and John Adams and Robert Redford, who lent their kind words.

Much thanks are owed to the photographers who contributed their artwork to the book, including Aaron Bennett, Francis Driscoll, Frank Knight, Mark McCarroll, and Thomas Teich. Similarly, much thanks are owed to those who assisted us in obtaining wonderful historic images from old black and white photographs and postcards from around the Catskill Park. These include: Evelyn Bennett at the Town of Shandaken Historical Museum; Helen Casey at the Delaware County Historical Association; Mark DuBois in Woodstock; John Dwyer in Platte Clove; Lonnie and Peg Gale in Phoenicia; Mark Loete and Stephanie Blackman in Chichester; Ruth Ann Muller and Gretchen Behl at the Olive Free Library in West Shokan; Cal Smith in Phoenicia; Carol Smythe, Town of Neversink Historian in Grahamsville; and Larry Tompkins in Windham. Karin Verschoor at the NYSDEC Division of Lands and Forests provided the modern map of the Catskill Park, and Kim Lorang of Visual Winds Studio scanned the historic forest preserve map.

Significant technical, editorial, and design contributions to the book were made by: editor Steve Hoare; designer Ron Toelke of Ron Toelke Associates; proofreaders Matina Billias, Natalie Mortensen, Eric Raetz, and Ed Volmar; and typist Dina Nester.

Many employees of the NYSDEC (and former Conservation Department) who are now deceased made invaluable contributions during their time to the development of Norm Van Valkenburgh's original accounts of the history of the New York State Forest Preserve and Adirondack and Catskill parks, which are recounted herein.

And, of course, we would be remiss if we did not acknowledge our deep appreciation for the support given to us by our families, particularly our wives, Dorothy Van Valkenburgh and Amy Olney.

The Catskill Park in Perspective

A man that I know who lived in the central Catskill Mountains his whole life was outside mowing his lawn one summer day. A car pulled up slowly and stopped. A Japanese man rolled down the window and said that he and his wife seemed to be lost. They asked, "Could you please tell us how to get to the entrance of the Catskill Park?" There was no good answer the local man could give to the visitors other than, "There *is* no entrance; you're already in the Catskill Park."

Why should the visitor's inquiry be such a hard question? It wouldn't be if it were in reference to just about any other state or national park in the country, or in the world for that matter. But New York's Catskill and Adirondack parks are unique and belie the conventional notion of what a park is. Here there are no gated park entrances with officials sitting in booths collecting fees and handing out park information. Unlike most parks in the United States, the public land in the Catskill and Adirondack parks is *not* one single, contiguous block of protected land; rather, the land enclosed within the park boundaries is a mosaic of both public and private land. A quick glance at any map of the Catskill Park and forest preserve is all that is needed to see the mosaic character of public *and* private land within the park, which is just one of many remarkable features of the Catskill Park.

Across New York State there are a variety of public parks and conservation lands, all with different classifications and management guidelines. State parks and state historic sites are managed today by the New York State Office of Parks, Recreation, and Historic Preservation (NYSOPRHP). State forests and reforestation areas, wildlife management areas, unique areas, special use areas, environmental education camps, public fishing areas, and the state forest preserve are managed by the New York State Department of Environmental Conservation (NYSDEC). The forest preserve consists of those state lands lying within the boundaries of the Catskill and Adirondack parks (with the exception of a few small parcels of "detached" forest preserve outside of the park boundaries), and the forest preserve is subject to much stricter protections than the other categories of public conservation lands across the state.

The 1,102-square-mile (705,500-acre) area of the Catskill Park lies in the mountainous area where Delaware, Greene, Sullivan, and Ulster counties meet in southeastern New York. The Catskill forest preserve is comprised of many blocky parcels of land, varying in size and shape, reflecting unique ownership patterns, odd lot lines, and the steady accumulation of relatively small state land acquisitions over time. In the core mountainous areas of the Catskill Park, these acquisitions have been aggregated over the years into some quite large tracts, while in other places there are still smaller, more scattered areas of forest preserve, all of it interspersed with private land and rural communities. The major units of state land in the Catskills are separated by valleys filled with roads, homes, businesses, small hamlets, and vibrant communities. Currently there are just over 285,000 acres of public forest preserve within the 705,500-acre Catskill Park; that is, approximately 40 percent of the land area in the Catskill Park is public, and 60 percent is private. Of the public land in the park, there are seven state campgrounds and even a state-run skiing facility, but most of the forest preserve lands are wild, forested expanses where Mother Nature is left to her designs, human improvements are minimal, and man is only a visitor.

The forest preserve encompasses a number of important ecosystems and habitat types, from extensive hardwood forests and spruce-fir summits to bogs, beaver meadows, vernal pools, and talus slopes. The New York State Constitution designates the forest preserve as "forever wild," and those lands are protected from sale, lease, development, and extractive industries. It is the forest preserve that contributes the essential element of wilderness to the overall mix of land uses that is the hallmark of the Catskill Park, and it is

New entrance signs commemorate the Catskill Park's 100th anniversary. (Mark McCarroll)

Road through Stony Clove, near the turn of the twentieth century. (Collection of Larry Tompkins)

critical to the overall setting and attractiveness of the greater Catskill region. The forest preserve is managed by NYSDEC for the preservation of natural habitat and ecosystem processes, and is made available for the perpetual enjoyment and recreation of the people of the state.

The fascinating history of the creation of the Catskill Park and forest preserve is as unique as the park itself. The New York State Forest Preserve, which includes lands in both the Adirondacks and Catskills, was created by law in 1885; these forest lands were some of the first natural areas in the nation to be protected by law. In 1864 the federal government granted the Yosemite Valley to the State of California as a public recreational and scenic preserve, but the land was not managed as wilderness and it suffered from exploitation for many more years. Yellowstone was designated as the United States' first national park in 1872 to protect its scenic and geological wonders, but it, too, suffered from abuses such as uncontrolled logging, mining, hunting, and degradation by souvenir hunters for more than twenty years afterward. The United States Congress did not create the Forest Service and a system of national forests until 1905, and the National Park Service was not established until 1916.

When the State of New York afforded the newly created forest preserve with constitutional protection in 1894, the state effectively created the nation's first designated wilderness area (even though "official" classification of certain forest preserve lands as "wilderness," and other forest preserve lands as other management types was not considered until the 1960s, and was not enacted until the 1970s in the Adirondacks nor until the 1980s in the Catskills). Establishment of federal primitive areas and a federal wilderness system did not begin to evolve until the 1920s, 1930s and 1940s, when championed by the likes of Aldo Leopold, Robert Marshall, Benton MacKaye, and others. It was not until 1964 that the National

Wilderness Act was finally passed (with a second bill in 1974), officially creating wilderness areas from portions of national forests and national parks.

It is little wonder that the precedent set by New York State in establishing wilderness areas was used as a model for designing the National Wilderness Preservation System, and that the champion of the federal wilderness system was none other than Howard Zahniser of the Wilderness Society (an organization founded by noted New York-born and educated conservationist Robert Marshall). Zahniser was greatly inspired and influenced by his experiences and time spent in the Adirondacks. In 1951 Zahniser stated: "It behooves us then to do two things. First we must see that an adequate system of [national] wilderness areas is designated for preservation, and then we must allow nothing to alter the wilderness character of the preserves. We have made an excellent start on such a program. Our obligation now—to those who have been our pioneers and to those of the future, as well as to our own generation—is to see that this program is not undone but perfected." Most maps depicting wilderness areas across the country show only these federally designated wilderness areas, leaving a seeming lack of wilderness in the east, and belying the fact that New York State was the forerunner in wilderness preservation.

The forest preserve we enjoy today was not created all at once in 1885. The amount of public lands protected by the designation of the forest preserve was small compared to today, and the nearly tenfold increase in

Catskill forest preserve since then is the result of over 100 years of active land acquisition work by the state. The early motives for forest preservation in New York were not purely altruistic or conservation-oriented, however. They were also fueled by economic interests focused on the maintenance of water power, water supply, and tourism. As will be explained later, the Catskills were almost left out of the picture when the forest preserve was created in 1885. They were only included because of shrewd political maneuvering to avoid taxes, and not for the more noble purpose of protecting land and natural resources. But the value of the forest preserve

Historic marker installed for the 50th anniversary of the New York Forest Preserve in 1935. (Chris Olney)

in the Catskills was quickly recognized and appreciated for what it was, largely because of the observations and advocacy of people such as Charles Carpenter, who wrote in detail about the problems and potential of the Catskill region. Carpenter toured the region and made extensive notes and judgments on behalf of the state forest commission, which he outlined in an influential

There are over 300 miles of hiking trails in the Catskill Park. (Collection of The Catskill Center)

report to the commission in 1886 (reprinted in full in Appendix A). For over a century the New York State Constitution has provided the protection that has perpetuated the Adirondack and Catskill forest preserve as one of the most unique examples of conservation in the United States.

When the Catskill Park boundary was first established and defined in 1904, it, too, was not done for any lofty philosophical purpose. It was created simply to help guide and focus state land acquisitions in the region. Unlike the Adirondack Park boundary, which essentially encompasses what can generally be considered the entire Adirondack region, the Catskill Park boundary is oddly shaped and contains only the central mountainous part of what might be considered the greater Catskill region. There are many areas of the Catskill region that lie outside of the park to the north, west, and south. Less than half the length of the Catskill Park boundary follows intuitive natural landscape features such as rivers or ridgelines, or even town and county lines. Why the boundary line is as it is, is largely a curious fact of history, but the Catskill Park has come to have far more significance for the communities that comprise it than originally intended.

At first the definition of the Catskill Park included only the state-owned forest preserve lands within the specific outlined area of the Catskills, but in 1912 it came to include both the public and private land in that area. This distinction has become another unique and special feature of the Catskill and Adirondack parks, distinguishing them from most others. Renowned Catskills historian Alf Evers has written that with the creation of the Catskill Park "the word 'park' took on an extended meaning to the people of the region," and "the new kind of park … was owned by the people and might be used by them except in ways that might damage the conservation goals of the park."

One could ask the question (and the question *was* asked several times in the early 1900s): "Should all of the land in the Catskill and Adirondack parks be acquired by the state?" Or analogously: "Should all of the land in the New York City Watershed be acquired by the city?" The answer, of course, is a resounding no. There is tremendous history and immeasurable value in the human communities that live in the Catskill Park. People have lived in the Catskills for hundreds of years, making the mountains their home or their playground, building communities, and making a living. The private lands of the Catskills give us places to live among the scenic beauty of the mountains and maintain our connections to the land.

Conversely, should we sacrifice the wilderness values of the "forever wild" forest preserve for economic gain or new places to live? Should we tap into the timber and other resources of the mountains that have been set aside for our benefit? Again, no. The intrinsic values of wilderness are many, and these forest preserve lands are a gift of nature that we have received from previous generations and are obligated to leave intact for future

generations. The former chief of NYSDEC's Bureau of Preserve Protection and Management, Garry Ives, stated in a forest preserve centennial article in 1985, "Implicit in the forever wild clause of the constitution is the corollary that the lands of the Forest Preserve constitute a precious environmental heritage and belong to all the people of New York." We can also ask: "Should all of the lands that remain in private ownership be subdivided and developed and marketed to accommodate the real estate demands of ever more people who want to live in this beautiful region?" There are, of course, no simple answers, but only a surfeit of opinions to these kinds of questions about future growth. Most would agree, however, that we must be diligent about not despoiling the primary asset that has drawn people here and continues to keep many of us here—namely, the scenic, rural character of the region.

The great value, appeal, and uniqueness of the Catskill Park lies in the mix of public and private land across the landscape, manifesting itself as untouched wilderness areas intermingled with working farms, forests, and small-town communities. It is the mix that forms a diversity of types of land cover in the region, benefiting many kinds of wildlife. Over the past few decades we have enjoyed the recovery of whitetail deer (in fact, now there is an overabundance), black bear, wild turkey, brook trout, bald eagle, fisher, and other species. It is the mix of public and private land that also forms a diversity of scenery and beauty in the region, benefiting the people who live here and visit here. The casual explorer will surely find that the beauty of the Catskills lies not just in the pristine spruce-fir summits, rugged rock outcrops, vast forest tracts, hidden lakes, bouldery trout streams, and graceful waterfalls, but also in the open hay meadows and dairy pastures, magnificent reservoirs, secluded homes in quiet hollows, undulating railroads, old barns and stone walls alluding to our agrarian past, and bustling, colorful main streets. It is all these things together and in close proximity to each other that give the Catskill region its charm and identity.

There are other reasons why this unique "patchwork quilt" pattern of public and private land in the Catskill Park is significant. For one, the scattered, intermingled pattern of land ownership creates many opportunities to meet the real estate demand for properties bordering protected land. With much of the state land so spread out, there is a much larger border, or "surface area," than there would be if the state land were consolidated in one contiguous block. The phrase "borders state land" is a strong selling point for many private properties because it allows many people to live on the edge of wilderness, close to nature. Villages and hamlets of the Catskill region are also spread out across the Catskill Park and this, coupled with the fact that there are numerous roads going into and out of the park with no defined Catskill Park entrance, means that for the most part there is no single "gateway community" that suffers from problems typical of such communities. Symptoms of gateway communities, such as sprawling commercial development and an overabundance of

tourist attractions, are relatively minor and diffuse in the Catskills, with one or two notable exceptions.

The Catskill forest preserve is an important draw for people seeking scenic beauty and outdoor recreation opportunities close to the great population centers of the state's Capital Region and Hudson Valley, as well as New York City, the northern New Jersey metropolitan area, and beyond. Recent estimates indicate that over five hundred thousand people recreate on Catskill forest preserve lands each year, and this number is thought to be quite conservative, with the actual visitation being significantly higher. Opportunities abound in the Catskill Park and adjacent areas for hiking, camping, fishing, hunting, snowshoeing, downhill and cross-country skiing, canoeing, kayaking, on and off-road bicycling, ice and rock climbing, snowmobiling, horseback riding, wildlife observation, nature study, and good old-fashioned sightseeing. These activities contribute significantly and directly to the nature-based economy of the region, bringing customers for the goods and services provided by local business owners. For decades the mountains have swelled with visitors seeking outdoor recreation, mountain beauty, fall colors, and cultural attractions. Many businesses in the region cater to the tourism industry, providing lodging, food, gas, shopping, art, and entertainment to travelers. The private lands, too, have measurable economic value, not just as real estate, but also in their production of timber, bluestone, and agricultural products.

But these measurable economic values are matched, and perhaps dwarfed, by other less tangible values—some also economic, and some of a more spiritual or philosophical nature. The larger, economically important values have to do with the "ecosystem services" provided by the open landscapes of the Catskill Mountains, which are hard to measure in monetary terms, but are crucial in maintaining our human society. These, of course, are things such as clean air and water. Few would dispute the fact that clean water is the single most important product that the Catskill Mountains have ever produced, constituting the daily drinking water supply for nearly 10 million Americans. The true economic value of that great resource is elusive, but it is in the billions of dollars. The fact that this water supply remains of such high quality is attributable to the fact that most of the water emanates from mountains protected by large tracts of forest preserve and intact private forest and farmlands.

The other major value of the mountains has to do with the philosophy of preserving large tracts of protected land as wilderness, as well as conserving private lands in a more managed, but equally valuable condition. Preservation of public wilderness ensures that there will always be places where nature can conduct herself with minimal interference from humans, thereby providing us with opportunities to learn continually from nature, find inspiration, and renew our awareness of our place in the natural world. Equally important is the conservation and good stewardship of privately owned farms and forests, ensuring that there will always be places where people can stay closely connected to the land. Keeping these undeveloped private lands intact means that there will continue to be places where we can live close to nature and teach

Hikers enjoying the view from Rusk Mountain. (Chris Olney)

our kids how to drive a tractor, stack hay bales, fire a gun, cast a fishing rod, gather the wood that keeps our homes warm, make maple syrup, and other skills and values that are becoming more and more scarce in our fast-paced modern world.

Today, beautiful views of mountains clad in a thick cover of forest await motorists traveling through such places as Stony Clove or the Peekamoose Valley, and they lie before hikers standing atop Giant Ledge, West Kill Mountain, or in the cab of the Balsam Lake Mountain fire tower. But it has not always been this way. Virtually the whole region was cut over and settled during the eighteenth and nineteenth centuries, with our forebears extracting the resources needed to build a growing young nation. Hardwood timber was cut, hemlocks were stripped of their bark, pastures were cleared to high elevations, bluestone was mined from the hills, and acid factories sprang up on many streams and dumped their poisons. Unlike the great conservation stories of the American West and other places, where dedicated people fought to save the last most important tracts of great wilderness, the story of the Catskill forest preserve is instead a story of wilderness lost and wilderness recovered. This is another fact that makes New York's forest preserve unique.

There are an estimated 65,000 acres of "first growth" forest in the central Catskill

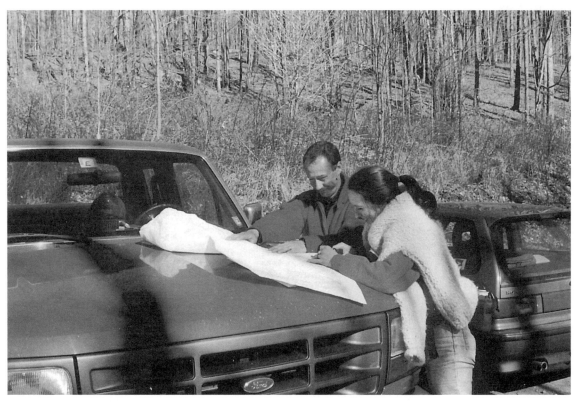

Forest Ranger helping a hiker with map and compass skills. (Chris Olney)

Mountains that were largely inaccessible and presumably never cut or substantially disturbed by man, according to Catskills forest history expert Michael Kudish. Most of the forests we see in the Catskills today, however, are fairly even-aged stands that have grown up from old pastures and clear-cuts. Most of the original Catskill wilderness was lost to exploitation, and much of it has subsequently been recovered through conservation and good private land stewardship. When the forest preserve was established in 1885, it consisted of only 33,894 acres in the Catskills, and there was still a significant amount of heavy resource extraction occurring on neighboring private lands (for example, the Fenwick Lumber Company operations on the flanks of Hunter Mountain during the first decades of the 1900s). The expansion of the forest preserve has been a long, gradual process of acquiring lands that were, for the most part, heavily used, and allowing them to recover and mature naturally.

Much was written in the twentieth century about the value of preserving wilderness. New York's own wilderness champion, Howard Zahniser, spoke well of wilderness in 1955 when he was fighting for a system of federal wilderness preservation:

It is characteristic of wilderness to impress its visitors with their relationship to other forms of life, and to afford those who linger an intimation of the interdependence of all life. In the wilderness it is thus possible to sense most keenly our human mem-

bership in the whole community of life on Earth. And in this possibility is perhaps one explanation for our modern deep-seated need for wilderness. … We deeply need the humility to know ourselves as the dependent members of a great community of life, and this can indeed be one of the spiritual benefits of a wilderness experience. Without the gadgets, the inventions, the contrivances whereby men have seemed to establish among themselves an independence of nature, without these distractions, to know the wilderness is to know a profound humility, to recognize one's littleness, to sense dependence and interdependence, indebtedness, and responsibility.

The fact that the wilderness areas of the Catskills are located in such close proximity to one of the world's largest urban centers and are accessible to so many people adds tremendously to their value and significance. This proximity of wilderness to such a huge population base is yet another important and unique aspect of the Catskill Park and forest preserve, and it creates management, stewardship, and education challenges that cannot be ignored. Many of the visitors who recreate in the Catskills need guidance on how to enjoy the outdoors safely without degrading the resource or negatively impacting the experiences of others. Mitigation of negative impacts caused by heavy use of campsites, trails, and other popular recreational areas is a continual process. Second-home owners and people who relocate here from urban environments also often need to be educated about rural ways of life and how to appreciate and avoid conflicts with their natural surroundings.

Landscape diversity is the hallmark of the region, changing in relative proportions over time, but always with the mix being more valuable than any one component. The mix of public and private, wilderness areas and intensive use areas, wildlife habitat and working lands, nature and people—all point to the Catskill Park's role as a living laboratory. The Catskill Park is certainly a grand experiment in how human communities can coexist with wilderness, geographically intermingled and historically entwined.

History of the Catskill Park and Forest Preserve

The history behind the creation and evolution of the Catskill Park and forest preserve is not fully understood by many. To learn the context of how the Catskill Park and forest preserve came to be, one has to look at what was going on in the Adirondacks and in the state Capitol during the eighteenth and nineteenth centuries.

In the early years of New York State, and indeed the nation, the state found itself the owner of several million acres of forested land. Following the Revolutionary War, in 1779 the new state's fledgling legislature passed what was referred to as the "Act of Attainder," a law officially transferring all lands owned by the Crown of England as of July 9, 1776, to the people of New York. The same act also voided the land titles of those who had remained loyal to the Crown during the fight for independence and declared those lands to be owned by the state. These lands amounted to approximately seven million acres and were mostly in the Adirondacks, covering that entire large region. In other parts of the state, huge tracts of land had been patented away by the Crown to individuals long before and were now mostly settled. This was especially true in the Catskills where Queen Anne had granted 1.5 million acres to Johannes Hardenbergh and his partners on April 20, 1708. The state therefore inherited little or no land in the Catskills when the Act of Attainder was passed.

There was no land preservation sentiment to speak of this early on in the state's history, and settlement and industry were the primary motivating social forces of the times. The young state government had little revenue to keep it functioning, and public officials seemed bent on getting rid of the millions of acres of land the state now held in the Adirondacks—a seemingly inexhaustible supply of natural resources. Early state legislatures, beginning in the 1780s and continuing for over fifty years, passed a series of laws designed for easy disposal of the "waste and unappropriated lands" of the Adirondacks. They sold off public land to private individuals for one shilling per acre, and exempted those lands from state taxes for a seven-year period. The single largest of these land grants was made to Alexander Macomb in 1792, when the state sold 3,635,200 acres to Macomb for "a generous eight pence per acre." Most of the buyers, however, were logging and railroad companies who were interested in turning a quick profit from cutting and selling timber. By the early 1800s the lumbermen had exhausted most of the easily accessible tracts in the flatlands and began to move up into the greener areas of the surrounding mountains. The state succeeded in getting rid of its Adirondack land, conveying nearly all of it to private interests by about 1820. Individual private landowners also often succumbed to the pressures of the logging companies, especially when they could no longer deal with the burden of property taxes. After the profitable trees and other resources were removed, the companies usually then abandoned the land and allowed the properties to return to the state for unpaid property taxes. Much of that land returned to public ownership far depleted in value after the removal or other destruction of the forest resource.

While the logging industry was the worst offender in the despoliation of the forests, other enterprises were also to blame. The tanning industry, especially in the Catskills, wiped out hemlock trees to the extent that tanneries were forced to give up the business because of the lack of readily available hemlock bark. The paper industry seriously depleted the spruce, pine, basswood, poplar, and white birch. The charcoal industry thrived on clear-cutting the area of its operation. Timber thieves stripped the unprotected state-owned lands. And of course the forests were further encroached upon by the settlements and farms that expanded into the interior of both the Adirondacks and the Catskills in the early 1800s. Those forests that were left on New York's mountains were often destroyed by major fires caused

by careless lumbermen, and later the railroads. Following a tour of the United States in 1831–32, French nobleman Alexis de Tocqueville wrote his observations and impressions: "In Europe people talk a great deal of the wilds of America, but the Americans themselves never think about them; they are insensible to the wonders of inanimate nature. Their eyes are fired with another site; they march across these wilds,

The NYSDEC maintains trailheads and other recreational improvements in the Catskill Park. (Collection of The Catskill Center)

clearing swamps, turning the courses of rivers." In the 1850s, the state legislature gave the railroad companies the right to purchase many thousands of acres of the remaining state lands, leaving only the inaccessible mountain peaks and passes.

The fish and game of the mountain regions were treated with the same careless abandon as the forests themselves. Early journalists and authors, after visiting the Adirondacks and Catskills, wrote of the seemingly infinite supply of sport that could be had in those areas. Stories of catching 120 pounds of trout in two hours, of shooting five deer in one month, or of catching a nineteen-pound trout were not uncommon and

Paddling on Waneta Lake. (Chris Olney)

were no doubt true, because there were no laws prohibiting such excessive harvests of fish and game. Tales such as these brought hunters and fishermen to the mountains in droves with the inevitable result that by 1820 the last trout was gone from Saratoga Lake; by 1822 the wolf had disappeared; the moose, elk, and panther disappeared; and no more nineteen-pound trout were reported. Hotels and spas sprang up in what forests were left, serviced by extensive new railroad systems, and by 1850 America's first wilderness was no more.

But popular attitudes about nature slowly began to change in the early to mid-1800s, and a romantic movement began to idealize nature and provide a voice to counter our culture's steady consumption of natural resources and degradation of natural systems. Famed painter Thomas Cole began painting idyllic scenes in the Catskill Mountains and Hudson Valley in the 1820s, and in 1839 Charles Cromwell Ingham, founder of the National Academy of Design, first exhibited his oil painting, *The Great Adirondack Pass,* inspired by a geology survey he participated in two years earlier. Such works began a tradition of Adirondack and Catskill landscape painting that would be popularized by the "Hudson River School" of landscape painters who followed in their footsteps.

Elliot Vesell, scholar of the Hudson River School, writes: "The work of the Hudson River School represents the first, and perhaps the last, systematic attempt to depict on canvas a unified vision of the American landscape. It celebrated the wonders of nature in this country by elaborately describing the facts of natural landscape and by presenting seemingly endless vistas through clear uncontaminated air." Vesell maintains that what the dozen or so artists of the Hudson River School shared was "a common spirit of devotion to nature and a common background of aesthetic ideas," and that their collective achievement in the mid-1800s was "to present a new view of nature and of man's relationship to nature which had widespread ramifications in American literature as well as in other aspects of American culture."

The paintings of the Hudson River School, along with the writings of authors and poets such as James Fenimore Cooper, Ralph Waldo Emerson, Henry David Thoreau, and Walt Whitman began to influence popular American conceptions about the value of nature. Vesell states that both the painters and writers of the early and mid-1800s generally "associated nature with virtue and civilization with degeneracy and evil," and summarizes that the basic message of popular nature-writing of the time was that "Americans, particularly close to nature, were still virtuous, but with the march of civilization as measured by the progress of the axe through the forests, virtue would vanish, health would be destroyed, and the nation's personality lost." Author Peter Wild notes that Thoreau was one of the earliest advocates for setting aside wildlands and leaving them in their natural state, and as early as the 1830s artist George Catlin was advocating for a system of national parks. A growing urban population began to embrace the

romanticism of nature and sought out beautiful places among the rivers and mountains to relax, recreate, and improve their physical and mental health.

The importance of forests in the matter of water supply began to be recognized in the 1850s. Water, of course, was necessary for drinking purposes, and for the lumbering industry and most other businesses of that time it was the least expensive and most convenient mode of transportation. Early naturalists and scientists pointed out that continued depletion of the woodlands of important watersheds seriously endangered the maintenance of stream flows and hastened flooding and erosion of valuable topsoil. Some early writers and editors in New York finally recognized that it was time for action and called for a new policy for the Adirondacks. S. J. Hammond, in his 1857 book *Wild Northern Scenes,* said of the Adirondacks, "Had I my way I would mark out a circle of a hundred miles in diameter and throw around it the protecting aegis of the constitution. I would make it a forest forever." George Dawson of the *Albany Evening Journal* said much the same thing in editorials of the late 1850s, and in an 1864 *New York Times* editorial, Henry J. Raymond asked that concerned citizens get together and "seizing upon the choicest of the Adirondack Mountains, before they are despoiled of their forest, make of them grand parks owned in common."

It was also in 1864 that George Perkins Marsh published *Man and Nature; or Physical Geography as Modified by Human Action.* This work is essentially one of the first textbooks on ecology, and in it Marsh describes the relationship of one part of the environment to another, and how the influences of man impact that relationship. Marsh singles out forest land in particular as critical for holding together other important components of a natural landscape. The book did not specifically address New York State; however, it became a foundation and influencing factor for others arguing for the New York State Forest Preserve in later years. People with scientific backgrounds gradually began to join the battle for forest protection in New York. Franklin B. Hough, a doctor and noted historian from Lewis County who, in 1881, became the first chief of the Federal Division of Forestry (forerunner to the Forest Service), traveled the backcountry of the Adirondacks directing the 1865 state census. He was appalled at the condition of the forests and was enough of a scientist to realize the disastrous results that could occur if denudation of the watersheds was allowed to continue. He began to preach the need for adoption of forest conservation practices, and he used his influence with friends in government to arouse public sentiment for his cause. Famed landscape architect and proponent of wild parks Frederick Law Olmsted also advocated the setting aside of land to protect the Adirondacks.

Conservationist John Muir and the Catskill's own nature essayist, John Burroughs, carried on the American popularization of nature in the latter half of the nineteenth century. Such authors, according to Peter Wild, "saw their souls reflected in America's wildlife and woodlands. To them, setting aside forests as unexploited wholes often took on a religious imperative. Their books and articles in magazines stirred the public to re-evaluate its long-ignored wild heritage." Similarly, sportsmen's groups and various hunting and fishing periodicals began the fight for a better system of game laws and game management in the 1860s and 1870s. Despite the formation of the Commission of Fisheries in 1868, the state's first natural resources-related commission, individuals eventually took matters into their own hands by buying large tracts of land and forming private fishing and hunting clubs. Trout-fishing historians Austin Francis (in his book *Catskill Rivers*) and Ed Van Put (in his book *The Beaverkill*) tell the stories of several such fishing clubs in the Catskills. Noted angling clubs such as the Willowemoc Club became established in 1868, the Salmo Fontinalis Club in 1873, the Beaverkill Association (later the Beaverkill Trout Club) in 1875, the Beaverkill Club in 1878, the Balsam Lake Club in 1883, the Fly Fishers Club of Brooklyn in 1895, and the Tuscarora Club in 1901. George Bird Grinnell, paleontologist, naturalist, and editor of the popular publication *Forest and Stream*, would argue continually in the final decade of the nineteenth century for sound forest management in the Adirondack forest preserve.

The economic motives of some of the powerful businessmen of the time were almost as strong for forest and watershed protection in New York's mountain areas as the motives of conservationists. Peter Wild notes that business groups such as the Manufacturer's Aid Association of Watertown were big supporters of the creation of a

New York forest preserve "because of industry's dependence on a steady supply of water power, which only healthy forests could provide," and that "business leaders in New York [City] recognized the link between the city's growth and nature. They fretted about sufficient drinking water but also about how to keep the Erie Canal full, their economic lifeline."

Verplanck Colvin, an Albany resident trained in law and a self-made land surveyor, first visited the Adirondacks in 1865 and "was amazed at the natural park-like beauty of this wilderness." He began suggesting the preservation of the remaining wilderness areas as a state park. On October 15, 1870, Colvin climbed Mount Seward in the Adirondacks and recorded that "the view hence was magnificent, yet differing from other of the loftier Adirondacks, in that no clearings were discernable; wilderness everywhere; lake on lake, river on river, mountain on mountain, numberless." It was at this place and at this time that the forest preserve of New York State started on the path toward reality. Following his trip, Colvin said in the Twenty-Fourth Annual Report of the New York State Museum of Natural History that "these forests should be preserved; and for posterity should be set aside, this Adirondack region, as a park for New York." No mention was made of the Catskills. The forest protection ideas of Colvin and Hough, who met each other at meetings of the Albany Institute (a respected literary and scientific society), were well

German Hollow lean-to near Arkville. (Aaron Bennett)

received by people who saw the need for a more reliable and clean water supply for Albany, possibly from the Hudson River, which emanated from the Adirondack Mountains.

The state legislature was paying attention to Albany's recent drought and water supply problems, and out of it all came an 1872 law (Chapter 848) that established "A commission of State parks ... to inquire into the expediency of providing for vesting in the State the title to the timbered regions lying within the counties of Lewis, Essex,

Old forest preserve boundary marker. (Collection of NYSDEC)

Clinton, Franklin, St. Lawrence, Herkimer and Hamilton, and converting the same into a public park." The commissioners, in reporting their results to the 1873 legislature, said, "we are of opinion that the protection of a great portion of that forest from wanton destruction is absolutely and immediately required."

The report outlined the scarcity of settlements in the area and pointed out the disastrous effects that mining, tanning, lumbering, and forest fires had had on what was once a vast tract of virgin forest. The report deplored the earlier sales of land to private individuals for nominal sums and the outright grants of huge tracts to railroad companies. It tabulated the public acreage in those Adirondack counties, which as of the date of the report was 39,854 acres, and noted that this was only a small fraction of the land holdings that had been vestd in the public at the conclusion of the Revolutionary War. The report elaborated that the State of New York contained some of the most remarkable watershed areas in eastern North America, with the St. Lawrence River on the north, the Great Lakes on the west, the Allegany River on the south, and the Hudson River on the east. The report did not recommend that the Adirondack forests be preserved forevermore, but it did recommend that consideration should be given to the utilization of the forests as a product or crop. It expounded on the value of boating, camping, hunting, and fishing "to strengthen and revive the human frame ... to afford that physical training which northern

America stands sadly in need of." It further pointed out the health-giving values of having a wilderness area accessible to a large population. It is worth noting that in this first official study the concepts of preservation, management, and recreational development were largely treated as compatible and simultaneously attainable.

Unfortunately, not much came of that report and opinion. In 1874, however, Assemblyman Thomas Alvord introduced a bill entitled "AN ACT to create and preserve a public forest, to be known as the Adirondack Park." The bill, though, did not have a Senate sponsor and progressed no further. In 1876, the state legislature did pass a law (Chapter 297) prohibiting "the disposal of any part of the public lands on Lake George or the islands thereof." In 1882 Governor Alonzo Cornell, in his message to the legislature, condemned the state's policy of selling its wildlands. He suggested that land uses in the Adirondacks should be carefully restricted. Similarly, Governor Grover Cleveland said in his 1883 message to the state legislature that the Adirondack forests should be preserved, and that the present state lands and all other lands "it may hereafter acquire" should be declared "to be park lands."

All of the pressure being brought about by public officials, individuals, and the public-at-large began to take effect in 1883. In that year the legislature passed a law (Chapter 13 of the Laws of 1883) prohibiting the sale "of lands belonging to the State situated in the counties of Clinton, Essex, Franklin, Fulton, Hamilton, Herkimer, Lewis, Saratoga, St. Lawrence and Warren,"

these being the seven counties inquired into by the 1872 commission, plus Warren County, which includes Lake George, and the two additional counties of Fulton and Saratoga. Another law passed that year (Chapter 470) also helped lay the groundwork for the future forest preserve, by granting the comptroller the authority to spend up to ten thousand dollars to purchase forest lands with unpaid taxes in the Adirondacks—the first such appropriation. The foundation for the forest preserve was being laid, but the Catskills were not going to be a part of it. *Or so it seemed.*

With the enactment of the laws stopping the sales of Adirondack lands, it appeared that the state was going to continue to be a major landowner. Furthermore, additional lands were coming to the state for unpaid taxes and through partition sales. The time had finally come to provide some sort of management and protection to its ownership. Accordingly, the deficiency budget of 1884 appropriated ten thousand dollars to the comptroller for "perfecting the state's title to such lands; of definitely locating, appraising and examining them as may be required; of protecting them from trespassers or despoilers and prosecuting all such offenders, and generally of guarding, preserving the value of and protecting such lands." The same budget (Chapter 551 of the Laws of 1884) provided five thousand dollars to the comptroller "for the employment of such experts as he may deem necessary to investigate and report a system of forest preservation." Here the Catskills now had a chance at protection because these "experts" were not confined to any single geographic area or list of specific counties. Furthermore, another New York-born and Adirondack-inspired conservationist, Theodore Roosevelt, made brief mention of the Catskills during the congressional debates about forest preservation. In 1884 Roosevelt told his New York State Assembly colleagues in a floor debate: "The effect of the destruction of the forests in the Adirondacks is already perceptible, but you can perceive the result of a wanton destruction of the woods far more clearly in the Catskills, where the destruction was greater. There they cut off all the woods. Almost all the streams dried up, and it is only now, when a young growth of trees is springing up, that a little water is beginning to run in the brooks again."

The "experts," or "commissioners" as they called themselves, were led by Professor Charles Sprague Sargent of Harvard University, the country's premier dendrologist at that time. The commission reported to Comptroller Alfred C. Chapin on January 23, 1885, saying that they had "devoted themselves industriously to the study of the question." They had visited the Adirondacks a number of times, had "caused a detailed examination of the position and condition of the Adirondack forests to be made by trained forest experts," and were convinced that something certainly did need to be done to preserve the forests. They noted the continued plundering in the Adirondacks that "reduces this whole region to an unproductive and dangerous desert." The commission

noted the advantages of a continuing forest on the flow of water and outlined the forest as a natural recreational area to be enjoyed by the people. It laid the blame for the destruction of the forests on the charcoal and lumber industries, the construction of numerous small reservoirs throughout the mountains, and forest fires. It pointed the finger of accusation at the railroads and loggers for the vast number of fires that were helping to destroy the remaining trees.

The commission experts had also "visited the forest region of Ulster and Delaware counties," but were not much impressed:

The forests of the Catskill region are not unlike in actual condition those covering the hills which mark the southern limits of the Adirondack plateau. The merchantable timber and the hemlock bark were long ago cut, and fires have more than once swept over the entire region, destroying the reproductive powers of the forest as originally composed and ruining the fertility of the thin soil covering the hills. The valleys have now, however, all been cleared for farms, and forest fires consequently occur less frequently than formerly. A stunted and scrubby growth of trees is gradually repossessing the hills, which, if strictly protected, may sooner or later develop into a comparatively valuable forest. The protection of these forests is, however, of less general importance than the preservation of the Adirondack forests. The possibility of their yielding merchantable timber again in any considerable quantities is at best remote; and they guard no streams of more than local influence. Their real value consists in increasing the beauties of summer resorts, which are of great importance to the people of the State.

The commissioners' report recommended that the state not enter into the acquisition of additional lands by condemnation, but rather needed to initiate an acquisition program based on purchases, which would be better received by the public. It stated, however, that there would be no benefit to purchasing additional lands if past poor management practices were to continue. The commissioners recommended that a forest commission be set up to create regulations and policy for the administration of public lands. The report went on to recommend legislation establishing a forest preserve of "all the lands now owned or which may hereafter be acquired by the State of New York" in the ten Adirondack counties listed in the 1883 law and the additional county of Washington, with such lands to "be forever kept as wild forest lands." A second law was recommended to amend the penal code to set forth punishments for violations relating to forest destruction, and a third law was recommended to provide that the lands of the forest preserve would be taxable for all purposes.

Horse and carriage on road up Slide Mountain, 1894. (Collection of NYSDEC)

The comptroller was willing to accept and endorse all of this, and to submit the recommendations to the state legislature for action. So the Catskills were still not intended to be included in the new forest preserve. But Comptroller Chapin had not fully reckoned with the likes of Cornelius Hardenbergh. The fact that the state land "now owned or which may hereafter be acquired" in the Catskills did become part of New York's forest preserve, and subsequently that a Catskill Park was created, all had to do with the tenacity of Hardenbergh and a complicated series of laws dealing with property taxes (and the nonpayment of them).

Cornelius A. J. Hardenbergh.
(Collection of The Catskill Center)

Cornelius A. J. Hardenbergh was a bachelor, farmer, merchant, and public servant. He owned and operated a 110-acre farm on the northerly bank of the Shawangunk Kill, at the point where the stream forms the southerly boundary of the Town of Shawangunk and the line between Ulster and Orange counties. He resided in Ulster County, but picked up his mail in Pine Bush, just across the "kill" in Orange County. Hardenbergh was an avowed opponent of taxes of all sorts. When a tax was to be imposed on his wheel-making shop and business in the early days of the Civil War, he closed his shop rather than pay the tax. An admiring public elected him supervisor of the Town of Shawangunk, and later he served on the Board of Supervisors of Ulster County, sometimes as its chairman. It was in this capacity that Hardenbergh became involved

in a running battle with Comptroller Chapin and his predecessors over state taxes being assessed on lands acquired by the county at tax sales. No matter that Ulster County was not being treated any differently from any other county in the state; Hardenbergh opposed such taxation by the state.

In the 1870s a succession of laws were passed requiring county treasurers to collect all taxes levied on lands for state or county purposes. These laws further required the counties to pay the state taxes by the first of May each year, whether the treasurers had been able to collect them or not. Ulster County was added to the list of counties subject to these requirements by Chapter 200 of the Laws of 1879. If that wasn't bad enough, Chapter 371 of the Laws of 1879 was passed a month later to restate, word for word, the same provisions that were in Chapter 200, allegedly enacted to correct a minor error in the title of the first law. If Hardenbergh wasn't incensed the first time around, he surely was at the passage of the second law. Then came Chapter 382 of the Laws of 1879, which provided that the comptroller would issue a deed to the counties for each parcel of land not redeemed or sold at the 1877 tax sale. That law further required that the counties were liable for the current unpaid taxes on these lands, as well as for later taxes that would come due. If the counties didn't pay the taxes in ninety days, then interest at the rate of 6 percent would be added.

The comptroller at this point was holding the winning hand. Hardenbergh, however, saw to it that Ulster County did not pay the comptroller's bills. He won a minor point when he influenced the passage of Chapter 573 of the Laws of 1880. This law restated the procedures for publishing notices of pending tax sales as such procedures had been set out in the 1879 laws. There was one change. The earlier laws had said, "the publishing of the said notice not to exceed the sum of two dollars for each newspaper so publishing each of the several notices." The 1880 law contained the same wording but added, "excepting in the county of Ulster, wherein the sum shall not exceed one dollar."

The next round also went to Hardenbergh. The last 1879 law had provided that after the state acquired title to unredeemed and unsold lands, the comptroller would deed these lands to the respective counties. Chapter 260 of the Laws of 1881 changed that for Ulster County only. This law said

that "should there be no purchaser willing to bid the amount due on the lot or parcel of land to be sold," then the Ulster Country treasurer could bid on the "lot or parcel of land for the county." He, then, and not the comptroller, would issue the deed to the county or, if so directed by the Ulster County Board of Supervisors, he could sell the land. Other provisions of this law clearly set out the battle lines. One section stated, in referring to the earlier laws, "Where any authority is given or duly enjoined by those laws on the comptroller of the state, the same authority shall be exercised and the same duty shall be devolved on the county treasurer of Ulster County." One of the final sections of the law provided that lands acquired by Ulster County for unpaid taxes "shall be exempt while so owned by said county from all taxes" and directed the treasurer "to strike such land from the tax roll." Finally, it repealed "All acts or parts of acts inconsistent herewith, so far as the county of Ulster is affected."

The comptroller won the round after that. Chapter 402 of the Laws of 1881 was passed just two weeks after Chapter 260. It repeated many of the provisions of an 1855 law on which all of the later laws had been based. While not ever mentioning Ulster County, the language of the law makes it clear to what county it was directed. The listing of counties required to turn over delinquent tax lands to the comptroller for sale, which did not include Ulster County, was followed by the phrase, "or any other county for which there may, at the time, be a special law authorizing and directing the treasurer thereof to sell 'lands of non-residents' for unpaid taxes thereon." That, of course, meant Ulster County. This latest law put things back the way they were. The comptroller was directed to issue deeds to the counties for unredeemed and unsold lands. The final provision of the law stated, "All acts and parts of acts inconsistent with the provisions of this act are hereby repealed."

The comptroller was still ahead with the passage of Chapter 516 of the Laws of 1883. This law set out what was to happen to the lands not sold in the 1881 tax sale. It included Ulster County, again not by name, but by the "all other counties" phrase. Again the comptroller was to issue the deeds to the counties, and the counties would be liable for taxes due and 6 percent interest if the comptroller's bills were not paid. In the case of Ulster County, they weren't. By this time, in fact, the county was in arrears some forty thousand dollars.

From his vantage point on the fringe of Ulster County, Hardenbergh needed someone "in high places." In 1879, the year when Ulster County began to run up its tax bill under the provisions of the laws detrimental to its interest, one of those representing the county was a freshman assemblyman, George H. Sharpe, from the City of Kingston. In that year all three assemblymen from Ulster County were freshmen, still novices at the devious routes of lawmaking. In 1880, when it appeared that Ulster County was on the verge of getting the upper hand, Sharpe had become Speaker of the Assembly. It was he who had successfully moved Chapter 260, Ulster County's high point in the battle,

through the legislative process. He was unable, however, to forestall the passage of Chapter 402. In 1882, a quiet year for Ulster County and its tax problems, Sharpe was serving his last year as an assemblyman and was no longer Speaker. He had, however, provided good service to his Ulster County constituency.

Another freshman assemblyman took his seat in 1882—Alfred C. Chapin, representing Kings County. He would later become the last mayor of the independent City of Brooklyn and would preside over its amalgamation into the City of New York at the turn of the century. Chapin was Speaker of the Assembly in 1883 when Chapter 516 was enacted, and he became comptroller the following year. It was he who would do the final battle with Hardenbergh, who was elected assemblyman in the November 1884 general election. Now Hardenbergh would carry his own bills, and he wasn't long in making himself known. Early in the session, influenced by the 1883 law prohibiting the sale of state lands in the eleven Adirondack counties, he introduced a bill to prohibit the state from selling its land in Ulster County also. It didn't get anywhere. Undeterred, he and his Ulster County colleague, Assemblyman Gilbert D. B. Hasbrouck of Port Ewen, went to work on a bill that was enacted on April 20, 1885—about the same time that Comptroller Chapin was receiving the report of the "experts" investigating "a system of forest preservation."

Chapter 158 was a sweeping piece of legislation. It repeated, by listing every one of the 1879, 1880, 1881, and 1883 laws, "as the same in any wise relate to the county of Ulster" and relieved the county "from the operation of said laws." It directed the comptroller to cancel all previous sales of lands to Ulster County under any of the repealed laws and to convey those lands to the state. Finally, and most importantly, it directed the comptroller to give credit in his books to Ulster County for the principal and interest due on the lands that would be conveyed to the state. In one law, Ulster County was out from under its debt, and its large tax sale land holdings were owned by the state.

Comptroller Chapin was supportive of the recommendation to create a "forever wild" forest preserve of the state lands in the eleven Adirondack counties. He even felt it only fair, as recommended by the report, that the state should pay taxes on these lands to the local governments where the lands were located. Hardenbergh had a particular ally in the Senate who also supported the creation of the forest preserve. Senator Henry R. Low, representing Orange County, was a near neighbor of Hardenbergh's, residing at Middletown, only fifteen miles south of Pine Bush. Low had been a sponsor of the original bill recommended by the experts and was a major participant in the conferences in which the final bill was written. He introduced the final bill in the Senate. The sponsor in the assembly was James W. Husted from Peekskill.

And so it was that the New York State Forest Preserve was created on May 15, 1885, when Governor David B. Hill signed Chapter 283 of the Laws of 1885. This law established a three-person Forest Commission "appointed by the governor by and with the advice and consent of the senate" to have "care, custody, control and superintendence of the forest preserve." The commission was empowered to "employ a forest warden, forest inspectors, a clerk and all such agents, as they may deem necessary." It stated (in Section 8) that "The lands now or hereafter constituting the forest preserve shall be forever kept as wild forest lands. They shall not be sold, nor shall they be leased or taken by any person or corporation, public or private." As had been recommended by the "experts," this law defined the forest

Laurel House above Kaaterskill Falls, near the turn of the twentieth century. (Collection of The Catskill Center)

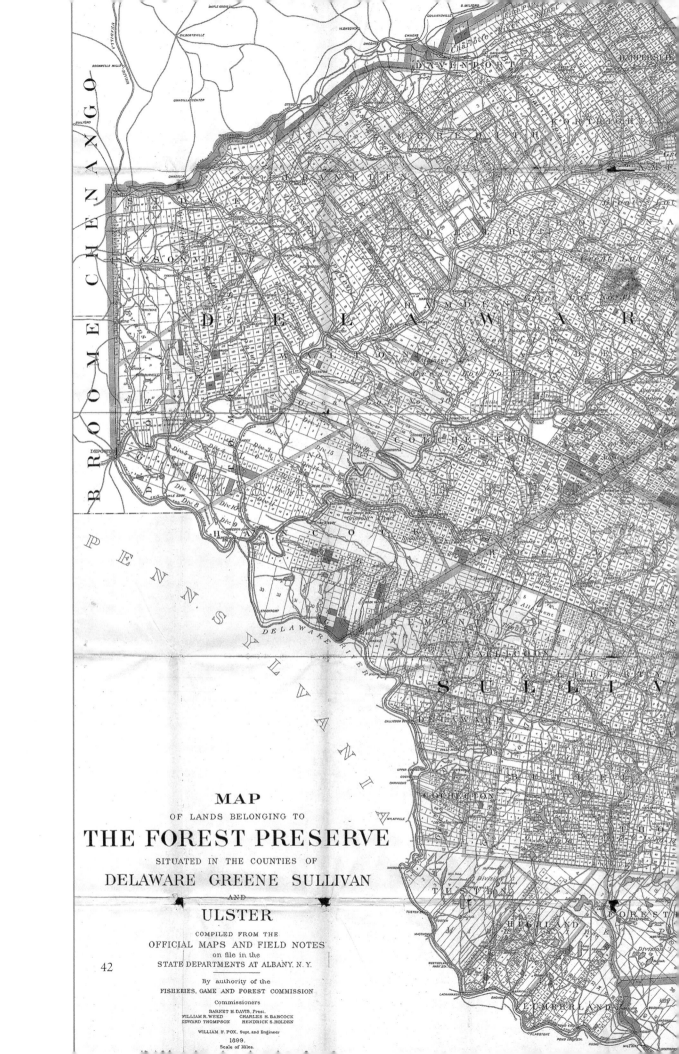

MAP

OF LANDS BELONGING TO

THE FOREST PRESERVE

SITUATED IN THE COUNTIES OF

DELAWARE GREENE SULLIVAN

AND

ULSTER

COMPILED FROM THE

OFFICIAL MAPS AND FIELD NOTES

on file in the

STATE DEPARTMENTS AT ALBANY, N. Y.

By authority of the

FISHERIES, GAME AND FOREST COMMISSION

Commissioners

BARNET H. DAVIS, Prest.

WILLIAM R. WEED   CHARLES H. BABCOCK

EDWARD THOMPSON   HENDRICK S. HOLDEN

WILLIAM F. FOX, Supt. and Engineer

1899.

Scale of Miles.

42

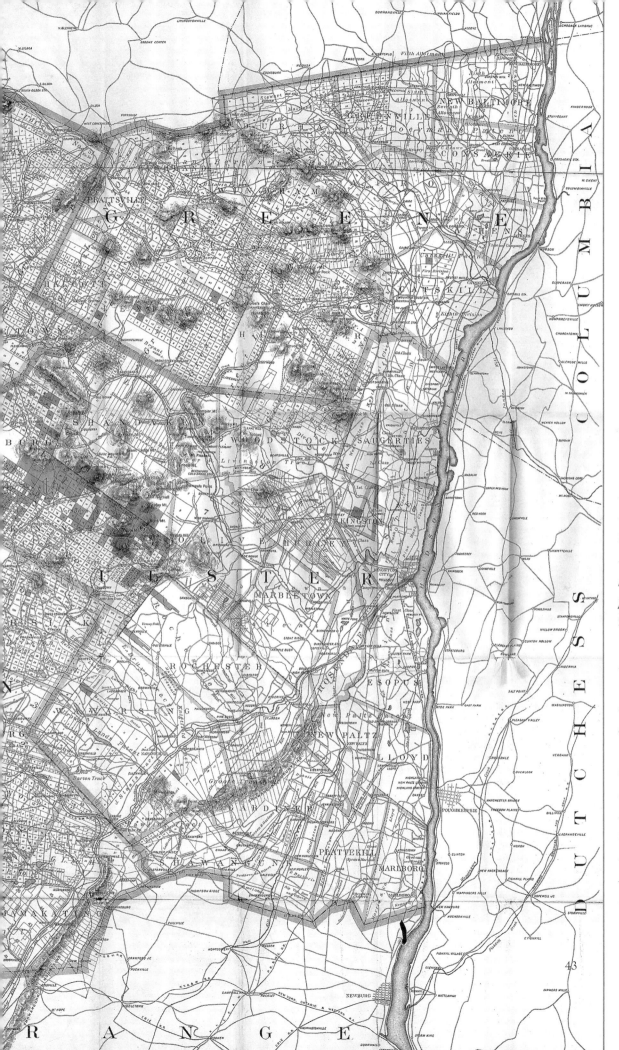

Map of Lands Belonging to the Forest Preserve, [dark-shaded parcels] Situated in the Counties of Delaware, Greene, Sullivan and Ulster, Compiled from the Official Maps and Field Notes on file in the State Departments at Albany, N.Y., 1899.

43

preserve as being "All the lands now owned or which may hereafter be acquired by the state of New York, within" the eleven Adirondack counties, except such lands in the Clinton County towns of Altona and Dannemora that were needed to provide land and a wood supply for the prison at Dannemora. Tacked onto the end of the list of Adirondack counties, thanks to the political maneuvering of Cornelius Hardenbergh, were the three Catskill counties of Greene, Ulster, and Sullivan. The forest preserve began with 681,374 acres in the Adirondacks and 33,894 acres in the Catskills.

Hardenbergh was serving the second year of his term when Chapter 280 of the Laws of 1886 was enacted. This was the companion bill recommended by the experts to provide for taxation of the state lands. It stated that all lands of the forest preserve "shall be assessed and taxed at a like valuation and at a like rate as those at which similar lands of individuals within such counties are assessed and taxed." It set out the procedures by which, and the dates when, the comptroller was required to certify, and the state treasurer was required to pay, annual taxes to the treasurers of the forest preserve counties. Thus, not only was Ulster County free from its tax bill, but from that time forward the county has received taxes from the state on those same lands that had been involved in the battle.

Hardenbergh left the Assembly at the end of his two-year term and went back to Ulster County. Over the years, many have debated just who was the "father" of the Adirondack forest preserve. The favorite

seems to be Verplanck Colvin, and rightly so. No such debate has asked who the "father" of the Catskill forest preserve was, however, probably because the Catskill forest preserve has just quietly existed without much controversy, and has therefore received less attention than its Adirondack counterpart. Those who know of Hardenbergh's involvement have debated his motives. Some say he was interested only in solving Ulster County's tax problems and took the way out offered by the times. Others say bringing the state lands of the Catskills into the forest preserve was his main goal and, in reaching that, he solved the tax problems. We probably will never know the answer, but the fact remains that whatever the motive, without Cornelius A. J. Hardenbergh the people of New York State would not enjoy the benefits of a Catskill forest preserve. That is certainly reason enough to remember his place in history .

It took a few months to appoint the three-person Forest Commission. The first appointment was quickly made a week or so after the signing of the law—Theodore B. Basselin, a lumberman from Croghan in Lewis County with one of the largest timber-cutting operations in the Adirondacks. It was not until September that the remaining two members were appointed—Townsend Cox, a New York City stockbroker from Glen Cove, Long Island, and Sherman W. Knevals, a lawyer from New York City. They held their first meeting on September 23, 1885, and "took immediate steps to familiarize themselves with the duties and various interests intrusted [sic] to their charge." The preservation of forests was their principal objective, for the stated purposes of ensuring "the value of present and future timber; the value of forests as 'health resorts'; the conservation of sources of water supply; the increase of rainfall; and the climatic and sanitary influence of forests." They visited the Adirondack and Catskill regions. These visits were cursory only, and they did not venture far from the main roads and villages. Instead, they hired "experienced, competent men … as special agents, who penetrated to every part of the wilderness."

In the case of the Catskills, the commission did not really know what they had.

After all, this addition to the forest preserve had been a last-minute political maneuver, and very little data existed as to the location of this state land asset. The commission recognized in its first annual report that "the existence of the Catskill Preserve seems to be little known, although the State owns a large tract in the Catskill region." A tabulation of the state ownership *did* exist, however, which indicated a total of 33,894 acres in the three Catskill counties. Greene County had 661 acres (507 acres in the Town of Lexington and 154 acres in the Town of Cairo). Sullivan County contained 502 acres (scattered in the towns of Highland, Lumberland, and Neversink). The remaining 32,731 acres were in

Hikers enjoying Wittenberg Mountain, early 1900s. (Collection of Lonnie and Peg Gale).

Ulster County (with most of that being in the mountainous towns of Denning, Hardenburgh, and Shandaken), principally on and around Slide Mountain. Most of this Catskill acreage was acquired by the state in the 1870s and 1880s as a result of tax sales and mortgage foreclosures. The commission was quick to realize that the listing of

Former observation tower on Kaaterskill High Peak. (Collection of Larry Tompkins)

Catskill counties was one short when they said "The Catskill region occupies parts of four counties," and it recommended a bill to add Delaware County.

The special agents who "penetrated to every part of the wilderness" came back with a different story from the experts who had previously reported to Comptroller Chapin. The Catskill forest preserve, they said, "is surrounded by the grandest of its scenery. Here the Slide Mountain rears its majestic form, surrounded by its retinue of lesser peaks. Here, also, are the deep, cool valleys, whose silence is broken only by the rushing cascades, or by the murmur of woodland sounds. Here are the rocky glens, among which the Peekamoose is so justly celebrated, while on every side the eye is greeted by an array of scenery unsurpassed throughout the State."

The streams also were "of more than local influence." The waters of the Schoharie Creek, they said, are "utilized as a feeder to the Erie Canal. ... The Esopus Creek ... pours its waters into the Hudson at Saugerties, affording an important water power, which is used to advantage by the manufacturers near its mouth. The east and west branches of the Neversink and the east branch of the Delaware all rise here, and flowing southward unite at Port Jervis and enter the Atlantic through Delaware Bay. ... Numerous mountain streams have become repopulated with trout, and now afford some of the best fishing in the State."

Even with that report, however, more needed to be known. In June of 1886, Commissioner Townsend Cox "penetrated" the interior of the Catskills himself when he climbed Slide Mountain, the tallest peak in the Catskills. While Cox's trip was largely for political reasons he did, in a meeting with reporters the following morning, stress the benefits of the Catskill forest preserve in maintaining the streams flowing from the area to form the rivers that were important to New York and its neighboring states.

In addition, the commission "detailed Inspector Charles F. Carpenter to make a thorough examination of the Catskill Preserve." Carpenter stood fourth in line in the hierarchy of the staff employed by the commission in 1886. Abner L. Train of Albany was secretary, Samuel F. Garmon of Lowville (Lewis County) was warden, William F. Fox of Albany was assistant warden, and Carpenter was the chief of two inspectors, drawing a salary of $125 a month. In addition, fifteen foresters were employed at $40 a month. All were headquartered throughout the Adirondacks except for one, Michael Hogan, who was stationed in Ellenville, Ulster County.

Carpenter did indeed make a thorough examination of the Catskill Mountains. His report covered fifty-one pages of the commission's annual report for 1886 (see Appendix A). He first described the geography of the Catskills, covering the mountains, streams, lakes, ponds, and soils. Then he detailed the forest cover of the area, deploring "the reckless waste going on all the time, and the noble forests mowed down to satisfy the cupidity of man." He talked about the state lands composing the new forest preserve, and he, too, thought Delaware County

should be added because "the State lands within that county are still under the control and management of the commissioners of the Land Office and the State Comptroller. While this state of affairs exists the people of this county lose the benefit of the act ... which provides for the taxation of State forest lands in the counties embracing the forest preserve." After all, he said, "the State paid a tax of $638.25 for the year 1886" to Ulster County.

Carpenter knew of the fight waged by Ulster County over its taxes because he discussed the various laws that had been involved up to and including the act that "passed April 20, 1885, just twenty-five days before the passage of the act creating the Forest Commission." All of it was, he said, "Through the enterprise of one or two citizens of Kingston ... an evidence of forethought and prudence, which from the earliest history of this region has always been justly attributed to the inhabitants of Wildwyk, now the city of Kingston."

Carpenter discussed the roads and highways and railroads that serviced the Catskills. He talked about the fine fishing and small-game hunting opportunities. He traced the history of the lumbering and tanning industries that had depleted the forests. He then described the "various industries" he had found "in making a tour of the counties embracing the Catskill forest preserve" town by town, village by village. He had, in fact, gone beyond the three counties, describing some industries in Delaware and Orange counties as well. He was impressed by the Catskills, concluding that he had "rarely found ... an abandoned homestead ... This distinguishes this wild region from the similar one in the Adirondacks, where deserted homesteads are met at frequent intervals, and in places the dilapidated remains of whole villages ... The Catskill region as a whole has a good soil and friendly climate, which the Adirondacks can scarcely be said to possess."

After all that, one would have thought that the Catskills would have received some major attention from the Forest Commission. But they didn't. The Catskills slipped into the role of being kid sister to the Adirondacks and would occupy that secondary place for decades. That situation has not always been all bad, however, as new ideas are generally tried first in the Adirondacks. If something works, then it is applied to the Catskills, hopefully with all the quirks worked out. One beneficial result from the initial attention paid to the Catskills by Carpenter and the first Forest Commission, however, was the passage of Chapter 520 of the Laws of 1888, which added Delaware County to the official listing of forest preserve counties and brought its 17,340 acres of state land into the Catskill forest preserve. Most of this land was south of the East Branch Delaware River and along the Ulster County line in the towns of Andes, Colchester, and Middletown.

Also at this time was the first real attack on, and weakening of, the newly created forest preserve. Chapter 475 of the Laws of 1887

redefined a part of the duties of the Forest Commission and authorized the commission to sell and convey "separate small parcels or tracts wholly detached from the main portions of the Forest Preserve and bounded on every side by lands not owned by the State, to sell the timber thereon, and to exchange these tracts for other lands adjoining the main tracts of the Forest Preserve." While this piece of legislation seems fairly definitive, it should be noted that no attempt was made to define the size of a "separate small parcel or tract." This law was presumably sponsored by the lumber interests, and it opened a crack in the door that had been slammed shut two years before. To some, it was a very poor and misguided law; to others it was made to order. Significantly, it became a statute without the governor's signature—he neither approved nor vetoed it within ten days, and therefore it returned to the legislature as law.

An Adirondack Park had been a concept talked about since the very first pleas for saving and preserving the Adirondack forests and mountains were heard. An 1864 *New York Times* editorial by Henry J. Raymond had said we should make "grand parks" of "the choicest of the Adirondack Mountains." Verplanck Colvin said, in speaking of the destruction of Adirondack forests in his 1870 report to the New York State Museum of Natural History, "The remedy for this is the creation of an Adirondack Park or timber preserve." The 1872 Commission of State Parks was to look into converting the timbered regions of certain Adirondack counties "into a public park." Colvin, in his 1874 report to the legislature on his "survey of the

Adirondack wilderness," talked about the state acquiring all of the land in the High Peaks region of Essex, Franklin, and Hamilton counties and setting it aside as a park. He continued to be the chief proponent of the Adirondack Park idea during the 1870s and 1880s.

Throughout these times, those speaking of an Adirondack Park envisioned that all lands within the park boundary would be state-owned public land. By 1890, however, that concept was beginning to change. Governor David B. Hill, in his message to the legislature of that year, thought a park should be outlined to include the "wilder portion of this [Adirondack] region covering the mountains and lakes," and then acquire lands in that park area. Chapter 8 of the Laws of 1890 redefined the forest preserve by re-listing all of the counties that had been set forth the previous year (which had grown from the original listing to include Oneida County in the southwestern Adirondacks), but then it excepted from the preserve all state lands within the limits of any incorporated village or city. Chapter 37 of the same year appropriated twenty-five thousand dollars to purchase lands in the forest preserve counties. It was the first such appropriation for the acquisition of lands to expand the preserve. This same law also made reference to a state park as it might relate to the forest preserve lands.

The Forest Commission report for 1890 called attention to the existing scattered pattern of state land ownership and recognized that additions to this state land must come from purchases. It noted the public senti-

ment favoring acquisition, and called for legislation to enable the state to acquire and hold state land in "one grand, unbroken domain." It stated that an advantage of increased ownership would be that greater

Legendary fisherman Ray Smith on the Esopus Creek, 1940s or 1950s. (Collection of Cal Smith)

Homestead in Bushnellville, date unknown. (Collection of Lonnie and Peg Gale)

control could be exercised against the railroads and trespass. The commissioners revised their reasons for preserving forests, which was now to be for the "maintenance of timber supply; conservation and protection of watersheds; preservation and protection of fish and game; and the founding of a permanent public resort."

Notably, the 1890 Forest Commission report included discussion on the subject of a proposed Adirondack Park. One of the most interesting parts of the report was the inclusion of a map of the Adirondacks on which a proposed park boundary had been delineated in blue. From that time forward, the phrases "inside the blue line" and "outside the blue line" have been used to describe lands inside and outside of the Adirondack and Catskill parks boundaries.

Unfortunately, the narrative of the report in regard to public ownership within a new Adirondack Park was contradictory. The commission seemed unwilling to say whether all lands inside the proposed park should be acquired by the state or not, so in different places in the text they said both. The report noted that it was unwise to proceed with acquisition of the entire Adirondack plateau; recognized the presence of villages and private clubs within the "blue line"; and concluded that proper forest management on private lands could be a compatible land use within the park. But at the same time, it said that all of the lands within the park boundary should gradually be acquired. There was also unclear language in regard to timbering on state lands inside and outside of the park boundary. The commission felt that state lands outside of the park should be sold whenever those lands did not, in the opinion of the commission, promote the purpose of the forest preserve, and that the proceeds could then be used to buy additional lands inside the park. The commission concluded by unanimously recommending the necessary legislation to establish and manage a park in the Adirondack wilderness, and state acquisition of titles to all the forest lands within the limits of the park "which it is possible to acquire, in the shortest practicable time." Use of the word "manage" would seem to leave the door open for the practice of forestry and lumbering on the state lands, and the use of the word "forest" as an adjective modifying the word "lands" suggests that it was the commission's recommendation not to acquire nonforested lands within the "blue line."

The 1891 report of the Forest Commission again addressed the idea of an Adirondack Park, and this time recommended a bill to create the park. Again the commission advocated for lumbering on forest preserve lands and for the sale of certain state lands outside the park. The report also referred to the sales of "separate small parcels and tracts" of land taking place under Chapter 475 of the Laws of 1887 (with one of the tracts sold in the Adirondacks being a not-so-small 3,673 acres). As far as the Catskills were concerned, the most important part of the report was a recommendation to provide fifty thousand dollars to acquire "forest land situated within the counties of Greene, Ulster, Delaware and Sullivan, at a price not exceeding one dollar and fifty cents per acre." The inclusion of funding for the Catskills, said the commission, was because the 1885 law "establishing the Forest Preserve, contemplated a reservation in the Catskills ... and not without good reason." This good reason was that state ownership was necessary to protect "the watersheds of our great rivers" and because "the wooded

slopes of the Hudson watershed demand special consideration." In making the first written reference to a Catskill Park, the commission said: "But there are other important reasons for the establishment of a forest park in the Catskills." These other important reasons were that the Catskill forest preserve "is in close proximity to the great cities of New York and Brooklyn and many cities along the Hudson. It is easily accessible to three-fourths of the population of the State ... It is a favorite spot with the vast population of New York and Brooklyn on account of its accessibility, cheap railroad fare, and desirable accommodations for people of moderate means."

Chapter 707 of the Laws of 1892 created the Adirondack Park and defined it to be "All land now owned, or which may hereafter be acquired by the state within" certain listed towns in the counties of Hamilton, Essex, Franklin, Herkimer, St. Lawrence, and Warren (a subset of the twelve Adirondack forest preserve counties), and stated that the state lands within the park were to "be forever reserved ... for the free use of all the people." Private land was not included in this first definition of the Adirondack Park, and the boundary was primarily for the purpose of specifying an area of the Adirondacks where state land acquisitions should be concentrated. The law repeated most of the provisions of the bill recommended a year earlier by the Forest Commission, including the authority to sell forest preserve lands throughout the Adirondacks (but not the Catskills), and also to lease lands for private camps and cottages. Governor Roswell Flower, in fact, thought that the state's judicious sale of timber and leases should pay for the maintenance of the preserve. The new law did repeal Chapter 475 of the Laws of 1887, allowing land exchanges. The law unfortunately did not include the previously recommended funding or authorization for acquiring forest preserve lands in the Catskills.

A minor consolation to the Catskills was Chapter 356 of the Laws of 1892, which provided $250 to the Forest Commission "for completing the public path leading to the summit of Slide Mountain, Ulster County, included within the preserve." Townsend Cox, still one of the commissioners, must have hoped the funding would put the "public path" in better shape than when he had traveled it back in 1886. An 1893 budget bill (Chapter 726) provided $1,000 "For the expenses of examination of title and survey of lands owned by the state on Slide Mountain in Ulster County and other parts of the Catskills." The $250 "public path" money may not seem of much importance, but it was the first legislation to authorize a recreational trail and is the point of beginning of the present extensive trail system throughout the Adirondacks and Catskills. The Catskills had a first after all!

The 1893 Forest Commission recognized that the $50,000 recommended for the Catskills in 1892 hadn't survived the legislative process. They didn't believe it proper to continue to discuss "the Adirondack wilderness to the utter exclusion of the interests of the Catskills." They thought some effort should be made to make "a solid tract of … these holdings … in scattered lots ... by the purchase of additional lands, in order that

they can be brought under some systematic management. ... We believe that it would be well to acquire 100,000 acres in the immediate vicinity of the lands mentioned." Accordingly, the commission recommended a bill to purchase "sixty thousand acres" in the Catskills "at a price not exceeding one dollar and fifty cents per acre." This recommendation, however, did not succeed either.

The Forest Commission and the state legislature proposed and enacted laws in 1892 and 1893 that liberalized, weakened, and capitalized on the forest preserve, allowing the leasing, timbering, and building of new roads on state lands. These facts did not escape the general public. The citizens of the state lost all faith in the legislature and the Forest Commission and became incensed over the increased mismanagement of the state's wilderness areas—surely the time was right for a new program to be established. Governor Flower was also disappointed with the current state of forest preserve affairs, unhappy with both laws and administration. He did not agree that public lands should be sold, and he advocated for a well-planned and well-funded acquisition program. He called for state controls on private lumbering and asked that administrators of the forest preserve be "active, capable and honest men."

The public reached the limit of its patience. In response to the repeated abuses in the management of the Adirondack forest preserve (such abuses were less common in the Catskills), which were mostly authorized by existing laws, a contingent of private individuals and organizations sought to ensure the perpetuation of the forest preserve by giving it constitutional protection. They planned to address the issue at the state's Constitutional Convention in 1894. In the early days of the convention, no mention was made of forest preservation and no committee was appointed to study the issue; however, behind the scenes some independent groups were at work on the issue. The New York Board of Trade and Transportation and the Brooklyn Constitution Club had opposed the forest preserve laws of 1893, but were unsuccessful in keeping that legislation from being passed. The groups then resolved to ensure meaningful preservation of the Adirondacks through the state constitution, and had the issue presented in Albany. They

outlined to the convention the various abuses that had been allowed to continue within the preserve, all of which were legal but certainly not in accordance with the wishes of the citizens of the state. They publicly announced that it was their intention to protect the forest preserve by having this protection made part of the constitution, rather than leaving it in the hands of changing legislatures and inept forest commissions. A special five-member Committee on State Forest Preservation, chaired by New York City attorney David McClure, was established to recommend action to protect the northern woods.

McClure and other contemporaries, such as Lewis County delegate Charles Mereness and Syracuse delegate William Goodelle, urged the state legislature to think of the protection of New York's forest land as an inexpensive and sound investment. They pointed

Dairy farm in East Windham, circa 1920. (Collection of Larry Tompkins)

to millions of dollars being allocated by the wealthy state for things such as improvement and expansion of the state capitol buildings, maintenance of waterways, and even World's Fair exhibits, but very little for forest preservation and the employment of wardens and foresters. They urged timely action to purchase and protect as much forest land as possible in the Adirondacks and Catskills. In his address to the Constitutional Convention, McClure stated:

> First of all we should not permit the sale of one acre of land. We should keep all we have. We should not exchange our lands—in an exchange the State is in danger of obtaining the worst of the taxing—and there is no necessity why we should part with any of our lands. We should not sell a tree or a branch of one. Some people may think in the wisdom of their scientific investigations that you can make the forests better by thinning out and selling to lumbermen some of the trees regardless of the devastation, the burnings and stealing that follow in the lumberman's track. But I say to you, gentlemen, no man has yet found it possible to improve on the ways of nature. In the primeval forest when the tree falls it is practically dead and where it falls it is a protection to the other trees; it takes in the moisture through its bark and rottenness and diffuses it down and into the soil … If our action here is practically unanimous, as I believe it will be, it will probably be followed by action on the part of the legislature looking to the purchase of more forest lands. We can buy those lands for a trifle …

Picnic by the Esopus Creek, 1940s or 1950s. (Collection of Cal Smith)

Finally, the legislature should purchase all of the forest lands, both in the Adirondacks and Catskills, not now owned by the State, and should preserve them, even though it costs millions of dollars to do it. The millions so invested will be well spent.

On September 15, 1894, the voting members of the constitutional convention passed the proposal for forest preserve protection under the constitution by a unanimous vote of 112-0. The forest preserve protection language was grouped with other changes suggested for the constitution, and in November the voters of the state passed the entire new constitution by a vote of 410,697 to 327,402 in the 1894 general election. A new Article VII addressing the forest preserve was inserted into the revised and adopted constitution and included the wording, "The lands of the state, now owned or hereafter acquired, constituting the forest preserve as now fixed by law, shall be forever kept as wild forest lands. They shall not be leased, sold or exchanged, or be taken by any corporation, public or private, nor shall the timber thereon be sold, removed or destroyed." These two sentences completely did away with every abuse that had heretofore been legally perpetrated on the forest preserve. The exchange of lands was done away with; the sale of state lands was stopped; the leasing of small camp lots was discontinued; no more railroad grants would be made; and the timber on the state holdings would remain forevermore. The new state constitution went into effect on January 1, 1895. From this day forward, decisions regarding the forest preserve

would be made by the people of the state, and each new law pertaining to the preserve would have to undergo the test of constitutionality. The people of the state had made certain that the administration of the forest preserve would be their responsibility and that any future decisions affecting the preserve would be made by them. Although not included in the controversies that raged beforehand, the Catskill forest preserve has enjoyed the benefits of this provision ever since.

A newly appointed Fisheries, Game, and Forest Commission (formed by combining the Fisheries Commission, Game Commission, and Forest Commission into a single entity) was empowered in 1895 to purchase additional forest preserve lands, but also to issue permits or leases for cutting softwood timber and laying out paths and roads. Thus, within a few months after the adoption of a constitutional provision for Article VII, the legislature was at work establishing the uses or concepts of forest and game management and recreational development, contrary to the basic concept of forest preservation in a natural state. It also took only a few months before the first constitutional challenge came along. In 1895 the legislature proposed a constitutional amendment to allow the leasing of five-acre campsites on lands of the forest preserve, the exchange of state-owned lands outside the Adirondack Park for private lands inside the park, and the sale of land outside the park to provide money with which to purchase land inside the park. This resolution was again passed in 1896 and then went before the people in the fall of that year, only to be defeated soundly by a vote of two to one.

It seemed the old fight between Ulster County and the state had not entirely faded away, or at least the solution to that fight had not been forgotten. By 1897, Ulster County (and other counties) had acquired additional lands under the tax sale laws of the times. Chapter 259 of the Laws of 1897 provided the means whereby the county could relieve itself of the burden of the ownership of these lands and the state could add to the forest preserve. The law directed the Fisheries, Game, and Forest Commission to examine the lands owned by Ulster County in the towns of Hardenburgh, Denning, and Shandaken "to determine what parcels of said lands it is desirable the state shall acquire and hold as a part of its lands within the forest preserve." The comptroller was directed to credit Ulster County for the value of the lands and interest at 6 percent from the date the county had acquired the land against any taxes the county owed to the state. Although only a minor amount of land was transferred under this law, Ulster County did clean up its last state debts. Cornelius Hardenbergh hadn't gone back to the Assembly, but the comptroller must have thought so.

With the advent of constitutional protection of the forest preserve, it became popular for the politicians of the day to advocate for the expansion of the preserve. The first funds for acquiring forest preserve lands in the Catskills were provided by Chapter 521 of the Laws of 1899, which appropriated fifty thousand dollars "to extend the forest preserve in the Catskills," and the first direct purchases of Catskill forest preserve land by the state were completed that same year (all in the Ulster County towns of Denning and Hardenburgh). Another fifty thousand dollars for the Catskills was appropriated in 1900. Also in 1900, Chapter 20 of the laws of that year reauthorized the establishment of "not more than three deer parks for breeding deer and wild game ... in the forest preserve in the counties of Delaware, Green [sic], Sullivan and Ulster." These "deer parks" had first been authorized in 1887. While only one such park was eventually established (on approximately one hundred acres near Slide Mountain), one wonders if it was in keeping with the preservation concept of forest preserve management that was embodied in the constitution. Further nonpreservation sentiments were instituted with Chapter 607 of the Laws of 1900, which provided funds to "appoint expert foresters ... who shall ... be employed in the work of reforesting the burned, barren or denuded lands in the forest preserve, and in such other work as may tend to the improvement ... of the state forest." The authorization to reforest the forest preserve was reissued again in 1910.

As the nineteenth century came to an end, the time for a Catskill Park was approaching. The first Catskill land map, however, published in 1899 did not include a proposed "blue line," or Catskill Park boundary. "In view of the repeated attempts to bring out this map, and the many obstacles and discouragements encountered," it obviously had not been as easy a task as producing the Adirondack land map, which by then had already been through a number of editions. The Catskill map delineated the various land allotments of the four counties, with the state lands colored in red and identifying "all the towns, villages, post-offices, roads, streams, and mountains." It would be helpful, said the Fisheries, Game, and Forest Commission, "in determining the areas that are best located for a further enlargement of the Catskill Preserve."

The reports of the various commissions and agencies of the time give no indication that a Catskill Park was even under consideration. Other than the single mention in 1891 (which may have been only a poor choice of words), all other writings were silent as to a Catskill Park. (This has frustrated officials of later commissions and departments when writing about the park and its beginnings.) The director of the Division of Lands and Forests (of the then Conservation Department), in reporting to the 1954 Joint Legislative Committee on Natural Resources, said, "the Catskill Park was created primarily for the purpose of delimiting those portions of the ... Catskill Forest Preserve counties embracing a portion of the wild forest lands and within which it was felt the land acquisition program should be centered." Two other Conservation Department papers of 1973 say much the same thing. One, entitled *The Catskill "Blue Line"*, says, "One primary intent of this boundary was to concentrate the future acquisition of Forest Preserve lands within this line. Some even envisioned that eventually the entire Park area would come under

Old-time Catskill entertainment, 1902. (Collection of larry Tompkins)

state ownership." The other one, entitled *Historical Background, Catskill Forest Preserve*, says, "One intent of the Blue Line was to concentrate purchase of Forest Preserve lands within these boundaries."

During the first few years of the new century, there was debate about the ability and appropriateness of the state in acquiring all of the lands within the Adirondack Park boundary (a debate which later could be considered in the Catskills as well). The 1900 report of the Forest Preserve Board went into great detail to show that it was not feasible to acquire all lands within the blue line. The most compelling reason given was that large acreages of the private lands were owned by wealthy firms and corporations that depended upon the land and its products to carry on their businesses, and that these owners would not sell to the state at any price. The board realized that it had the power to acquire the lands by appropriation, but stated that it was unwilling to do so because of the large claim that would be submitted by the owner as a result. The board stated, "Under condemnation, the owner of forest land would undoubtedly include in the claim for damages the loss of his mills and other idle plant, which would become worthless when his supply of raw material is thus cut off. Hence to the cost of the lands must be added the millions of dollars invested in mills and plants dependent on these lands, property which must be bought as well as the forest."

Governor Benjamin Odell, in his 1902 message to the legislature, suggested that the outright acquisition of all of the land within the Adirondack Park boundary under existing laws was not realistic or economically feasible. The governor noted that private ownerships within the Adirondack Park amounted to nearly 2 million acres, and estimated the value to be more than $5 million. He proposed that the law could be amended to allow individuals and corporations the right to sell land to the state and retain the timbering rights, thereby making it possible for the state to acquire land at less expense. The Forest, Fish, and Game Commission (renamed in 1900 from the Fisheries, Game, and Forest Commission) felt more optimistic that almost all of the lands within the park could be obtained and that "it would be well if the State kept a fund on hand, avail-

able at all times, for the purchase of such tracts whenever any portion is available upon the market." Governor Odell changed his tune in 1904 and stated his belief that "the State should eventually own every acre of land within the preserve," and that "in every private camp ... at least the timber rights should be secured through purchase or condemnation."

The Forest Commission, and the succeeding Fisheries, Game, and Forest Commission and Forest, Fish, and Game Commission, had not been happy about placing the forest preserve under the protection of the state constitution. The commissioners and their staff felt, at the very least, that provision should be made to allow for the sale of some of the less desirable parcels of forest preserve. Whether cued by statements to that effect in the annual reports of those commissions or not, the Senate appointed (using a long name, as was popular in that day) a Special Committee of the Senate on the Future Policy of the State in Relation to the Adirondacks and Forest Preservation. The answer to the Catskill Park is in the pages of the February 1904 report of that obscure committee.

The committee found that "the state is the owner of approximately 135,000 acres of lands lying in detached parcels ranging from 10 to 500 acres in counties in the Forest Preserve, but outside the [Adirondack] Park limits, and for the most part wholly unsuited for a forest preserve." It recognized that the constitution prevented the sale of such lands and recommended an amendment to permit such sales, but only for those parcels "outside of the park limits" that were "unsuited" to be a part of the forest preserve. The committee realized that would solve only a part of the detached-parcel problem, because the constitution covered the Catskills "where no park has yet been laid out." To remedy that, they said, "As soon as the boundaries of such a park can be established by legislative enactment, parcels of lands in those counties beyond its limits should likewise be disposed of." Thus, the Catskill Park was established not for what was in it or what was to be done within it, but rather for what was outside of it.

In concluding its report with a listing of its recommended actions for a constitutional amendment, the commission asked for "The passage of an act defining the boundaries of the Catskill Park." The recommended amendment to the constitution was introduced and passed in the 1904 Senate and Assembly, but was not taken up again. (A similar amendment was introduced in the 1907 Senate, but no further action was taken.) However, Chapter 233 of the Laws of 1904 was approved by the governor, and on April 5, 1904, the Catskill Park was created. The law stated, "The Catskill Park shall include all lands now owned or hereafter acquired by the state within the following boundaries"; and was then defined with a metes-and-bounds description of the new park, unlike the first description of the Adirondack Park. As in the Adirondacks, private land was not included in the first definition of the Catskill Park. The law concluded by saying, "Such park shall forever be reserved and maintained for the free use of all the people."

The new Catskill Park "blue line" inscribed and included part of the towns of Middletown, Andes, and Colchester in Delaware County; all of the Town of Jewett and part of the towns of Lexington, Prattsville, Ashland, Windham, Durham, Cairo, Catskill, and Hunter in Greene County; part of the towns of Rockland and Neversink in Sullivan County; and all of the towns of Hardenburgh, Denning, and Shandaken and part of the towns of Woodstock, Saugerties, Olive, Rochester, and Wawarsing in Ulster County (see map on page 60). The idea was to include the high mountains and "every part of the wilderness" area of the Catskills. The new park boundary encompassed a total of 576,120 acres within its boundary, and the Catskill forest preserve by this time had grown to over 92,000 acres.

A month later, Chapter 717 of the Laws of 1904 provided fifty thousand dollars "for the purpose of acquiring land in the Catskill Park ... but no part of such money shall be applicable to the purchase of lands without

Camping in the Rondout Valley, 1908.
(Collection of the Town of Neversink)

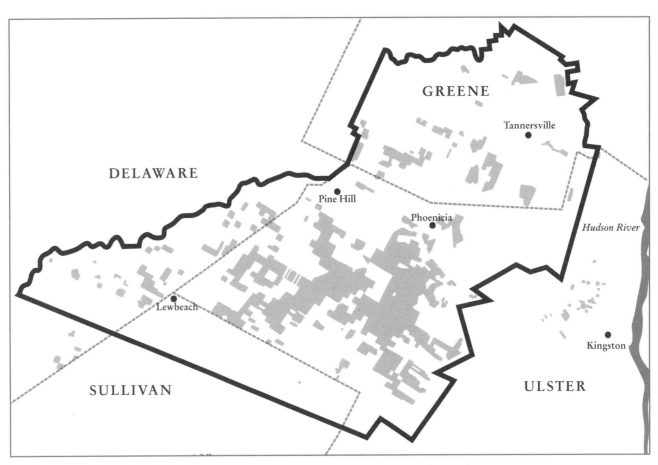

The Catskill Park blue line, 1904–1957. Shaded areas indicate forest preserve circa 1920. (Adapted from map in NYSDEC Collection)

the limits of such park as established by law in the year nineteen hundred and four." This gives some substance to the thinking that the park was created to define an area in which the state would concentrate its land acquisitions for forest preserve purposes. Most of the early state acquisitions in the Catskills were small and scattered compared to those in the Adirondacks, but a strong foundation for the forest preserve was being adequately laid. Many of the acquisitions in the first years of the century were on the northerly slopes of Slide Mountain and along the Esopus Valley near Oliverea, but also includ-

ed the entire east slopes of Stony Clove and a number of remote parcels in Hardenburgh.

Not much ado at all was made about the designation of the Catskill Park. The 1905 report of the Forest, Fish, and Game Commission said only, "The Catskill Park, as defined in the State law, contains 576,120 acres, and includes a part of each of the following named counties: Delaware, Greene, Sullivan and Ulster." Apparently to make up for the lack of attention given to the subject, it said the same thing, word for word, in another section of the report. The 1906 report said even less. It only noted that the state then owned 94,468 acres of land "within the Catskill Park" and 10,056 acres outside the park. From then until it was enlarged in 1957, the Catskill Park seemed to just be there. It excited few, and caused no problems. The succeeding commissions and departments did concentrate their forest preserve land acquisitions inside of the park.

✿ ✿ ✿

The first official state forest fire observation tower was built in the Catskill Mountains in 1905, in response to several years of devastating fires beginning with an intense drought in 1903. The tower was erected on the summit of Balsam Lake Mountain and replaced a log observatory that had been built there by the Balsam Lake Club in 1887. Another fifty thousand dollars was approved for forest preserve acquisitions in the Catskills in 1906. In 1909 two more fire observation towers were added in the Catskills—one on the summit of Belleayre Mountain and one on the summit of Hunter Mountain—and in 1912 another tower was placed on the summit of Slide Mountain. During his tenure in the New York State Senate from 1910 until 1913, Franklin D. Roosevelt was chairman of the Senate's Forest, Fish, and Game Committee. Roosevelt's strong conservation convictions as New York State governor and president of the United States were fortified by his early experiences fighting for improvements to natural resources management as a New York State senator. In 1922 he was a founding

board member of what would become the state's leading outdoor recreation organization, the Adirondack Mountain Club.

Chapter 444 of the Laws of 1912 changed the lead wording of the description of the Catskill and Adirondack parks to read,

Hunter Mountain fire tower, 1909.
(Collection of NYSDEC)

"All lands located ... within the following described boundaries," to now include the private lands as well as the state lands in the park designation. At the time, this was an insignificant change with no real purpose, but years later it would come to have significant ramifications, especially in the Adirondacks where the Adirondack Park Agency would be created to control and limit some uses and development of private lands inside the park. In 1913 the state constitution was amended to allow up to 3 percent of the total forest preserve acreage to be used for water reservoirs for the purposes of municipal water supplies, state canals, and stream regulation. In 1923, however, the voters of the state would defeat a proposed amendment to allow forest preserve land to be used for hydroelectric purposes, and in 1953 an amendment would be passed to revise the 1913 amendment to disallow the control and regulation of stream flows on forest preserve lands.

The year 1915 saw another Constitutional Convention, this one with much active debate about the forest preserve. There was significant pressure to give greater management latitude to the Conservation Commission (formerly the Forest, Fish, and Game Commission, renamed in 1911), with the logging industry very vocal about promoting increased management of the forest preserve. With the advent of the automobile, there was also pressure to open up several areas of forest preserve to motor vehicle access. On the flip side, however, were many preservationists who argued in defense of the "forever wild" clause of the constitution. The

noted New York lawyer and conservationist Louis Marshall, father of the famed Forest Service reformer and national wilderness advocate Robert Marshall, was one of those during the convention who fought against the interests of powerful lumber companies and for the protection of the wilderness values of the forest preserve. Louis Marshall had also been a voting member of the 1894 Constitutional Convention, when the forest preserve formally received its "forever wild" protection under the state constitution. In the end, the arguments of the lumber interests and liberal-management proponents were rejected by the delegates in their final vote—perhaps the strongest indication on record since 1872 that wild forest lands were intended to be touched by man as little as possible, and that the concept of preservation was intended to be placed above either "management" or "recreational development." Constitutional conventions in 1938 and 1967 would also threaten the forest preserve's constitutional protections as wilderness, and would also fail.

After a few years of criticism over inadequate yearly appropriations for land acquisitions and inactivity in soliciting important landowners, a law was passed in 1916 (Chapter 569) to provide for the issuance of bonds in the amount of $10 million "for the acquisition of lands for state park purposes." Of the total, $7.5 million was to be made available for additions to the Adirondack and Catskill forest preserves. The Association for the Protection of the Adirondacks, a nonprofit organization that had formed in 1902 to safeguard the Adirondack and Catskill forest preserve, was instrumental in gaining public support and acceptance for the bond issue. They were assisted in their efforts by the state's Conservation Commission. The referendum was approved by a vote of 650,349 to 499,853; it was the first in a series of bond acts that have helped to significantly expand the forest preserve throughout the twentieth century.

Several reasons were given to justify the expenditure of the additional money on forest preservation: 1) for the protection of existing forest preserve; 2) for watershed protection; 3) for soil conservation; 4) for climatological effects; 5) for recreational and health purposes; 6) for the preservation of scenic beauty; 7) for the consolidation of existing state holdings; and 8) for promotion of the local economy. The Association for the Protection of the Adirondacks advocated, and the state Conservation Commission adopted, a prioritization scheme for land acquisitions under the bond act funds. The first lands to be purchased would be mountaintops and steep mountain slopes, especially those where lumbering could severely impair the forest cover and scenic qualities. The second most important areas to acquire were lands where extensive hardwood lumbering was being conducted. Third were lumbered lands where the forest fire risks were negligible; fourth were other recently

Phoenicia—a community amidst the mountains, date unknown. (Collection of Lonnie and Peg Gale)

lumbered lands; and last were lands that had been burned over, but were suitable for reforestation.

It took until 1927 to spend all of the $7.5 million provided by the 1916 bond act. Of the 413 acquisitions that were made, 341 were by willing sellers and 72 were by appropriation or condemnation. The acquisitions added 245,000 acres to the Adirondack forest preserve and nearly 49,000 acres to the Catskill forest preserve. Acquisitions in the Catskills centered on the high peaks with all or parts of Hunter, West Kill, Kaaterskill High Peak, Tremper, Blackhead, Thomas Cole, Plateau, Twin, Sugarloaf, Indian Head, and Belleayre mountains being brought into the public domain. Major purchases were also made in Stony Clove, Kaaterskill Clove, and Platte Clove. Nearly 33,000 acres of the total added to the Catskill forest preserve were in the Esopus Creek and Schoharie Creek watersheds, helping to ensure a safe

Devil's Kitchen tollbooth, Platte Clove, circa 1895–1900. (Collection of John Dwyer)

and clean future water supply for New York City. Another forest fire observation tower was erected atop Tremper Mountain in 1917, and one on Red Hill in 1920.

For all that, the legislature continued to pass laws that were clearly in conflict with the constitutional "forever wild" provision. Chapter 401 of the Laws of 1921 authorized "the state commission of highways to use stone, gravel and sand and to occupy a right of way on certain lands in the forest preserve in order to construct the state and county highways designated" in the law. Chapter 275 of the Laws of 1924 expanded the provisions of the 1921 law to allow the use of stone, gravel, and sand from the forest preserve, and to occupy a right of way over the forest preserve "as … necessary to construct, maintain or reconstruct the state and county highways which have been heretofore improved, or which may hereafter be designated by law." A second law added language allowing a specific highway to be constructed in the Adirondacks.

In 1924 a second bond issue was passed, this time for $15 million with $5 million specified for land purchases "within or without the limits of the Adirondack and Catskill Parks." Again, purchases were designed to "protect steep slopes of forested mountains" and "forest which might be lumbered where consequent to such operations, there will be an unusual fire risk" and also to "reduce administrative expenses and consolidate ownership," "maintain and increase the health, recreational and game interests," and "reduce the cost of litigation in protecting the State's title to land in dispute." It was not advocated

that these funds be expended with the goal of achieving state ownership of all of the lands within the park boundaries. It was reasoned, in fact, that state acquisitions should be made while recognizing that alternating public and private ownerships within the parks was good and should be continued.

Once again it took many years to carry out the acquisition program and spend all of the allotted funds. It was not until 1944 that the program was officially closed, with a final report indicating 509 separate acquisitions adding 272,000 acres to the Adirondack forest preserve and over 72,000 acres to the Catskill forest preserve. The average cost of land in the Catskills at this time was $9.59 per acre. Most acquisitions were small and designed to consolidate existing landholdings. One notable purchase made in 1930 was 2,197 acres, at a total cost of $26,375, from Catskill Mountain House Inc., which included all of North Lake and much of the Catskill Mountain House property in Greene County. In 1926 the state opened its first two public campsites (now called "campgrounds") in the Catskill Park, one at a site known as Devil's Tombstone in Stony Clove, in the Town of Hunter, and one in Woodland Valley, in the Town of Shandaken. The Beaverkill Campsite, in the Town of Rockland, was added in 1928, and the North Lake Campsite (now called North-South Lake Campground), in the Town of Hunter, in 1930. Campground facilities, trails, and other recreational improvements were built with the valuable assistance of the Civilian Conservation Corps in the 1930s. The first state publication on Catskill trails was released in 1928 by the Conservation Department (formerly the Conservation Commission, renamed in 1927).

The Conservation Department started a program under the authority of Chapter 195 of the Laws of 1929 to acquire lands across the state for the establishment of reforestation areas. The program, because of the provisions of the constitution, excluded the four Catskill and twelve Adirondack counties; however, most agreed that lands inside the counties but outside the two park boundaries were suitable for reforestation purposes. With the advent of the new program, these fringe areas would become a no-man's-land, with the department restricting its forest preserve land acquisitions to within the parks. Accordingly, an amendment was proposed and approved in the 1931 general election to provide "for the acquisition by the state of land, outside the Adirondack and Catskill parks, as now fixed by law, best suited for reforestation, for the reforesting of the same and the protection and management of forests thereon." While this gave an added purpose to the park it was, again, for the reason of what was outside rather than what was inside. The 1931 amendment also put the Catskill and Adirondack parks in the wording of the state constitution for the first time. After that brief recognition, the Catskill Park reverted to obscurity once again. In 1932 the so-called "recreation amendment" was defeated by a vote of over two to one. This proposal would have allowed the state to construct paths, trails, campsites, and camping facilities on the forest preserve, and to make the "necessary clearings of timber

therefore." The fact of the defeat of this proposal calls into question the constitutionality of the public campsites then, and now, on the forest preserve, and the many miles of paths and trails that wind their way through these state lands.

The fifty-year anniversary of the state forest preserve was celebrated in 1935; included were a number of ceremonies across the state and a visit to the Adirondacks by President Franklin D. Roosevelt. 1935 was also the year the debate was revisited as to how much land within the Adirondack and Catskill parks should be acquired by the state. The State Planning Board said in a comprehensive plan that "as the state's finances permit, the purchase of forest preserve should be continued, until about 75 per cent of the park area is in state ownership." In 1940 the $5 million bond act money was nearly depleted. The Conservation Department recommended further funding and suggested that a definite policy be established to fix a limit on the expansion of the forest preserve. Individual yearly appropriations were common over the next couple of decades, but there were no more bond acts until 1960. In total, these funding measures did not approach the grand sums of the past bond issues, or those that would follow. They did, however, allow the representatives of the Conservation Department to be selective about their acquisitions, and since funds were not guaranteed, landowners were less likely to try to wait for rising land values before selling. Important acquisitions in the Catskills during this period included substantial areas along the Esopus Creek and the east and west branches of the Neversink Creek, as well as the single large purchase of 1,310 acres around and including Mongaup Pond in Sullivan County (the largest water body in the Catskill Park, not including the New York City water-supply reservoirs).

In 1938 the state constitution was recodified. Article VII, which had addressed the state forest preserve since 1894, became Article XIV, and remains so today. In 1947 the constitution was amended, after a public vote of 1,400,000 for and 830,000 against, to create the state-run Belleayre Ski Area on Belleayre Mountain in the Town of Shandaken as an economic stimulus initiative for the rural Catskill region. The amendment permitted the construction of up to twenty miles of downhill ski trails, thirty to eighty feet wide, on forest preserve lands. The maximum mileage and width of the ski trails would later be increased by another constitutional amendment in 1987, allowing for Belleayre's expansion to stay economically viable and competitive with other regional ski areas. In 1950 the network of fire observation towers in the Catskill Park was expanded to include a new tower on Overlook Mountain near Woodstock.

In 1952, at the request of the Conservation Department, the Joint Legislative Committee on Natural Resources undertook a study of the forest preserve, seeking to set the future policy of its management in the Adirondacks and Catskills. This committee

Skiers at the former Simpson Ski Slope, 1930s or 1940s. (Collection of Lonnie and Peg Gale)

established a Special Advisory Committee on the Forest Preserve and charged it with looking into a number of subjects, one being the so-called detached parcels of forest preserve situated within the forest preserve counties but outside the Adirondack and Catskill park boundaries. Most of these parcels were small and isolated and had been acquired by the department in the 1920s as the result of laws then requiring that the state acquire from the forest preserve counties those lands that the counties had acquired through tax sales. The department had no idea where these parcels were, for the most part, and therefore they were often of little value for public use. For example, it was common practice among the department's land surveyors, when called upon to survey one of these parcels, to look around the general area in which a detached parcel was supposed to be located and find where the local residents were dumping their garbage. Chances are, they said, that would be the state-owned lot, and it usually was.

Following an in-depth study of these detached forest preserve parcels, the Joint Legislative Committee introduced two constitutional amendments in 1956. The first amendment would have provided that the legislature could dedicate detached parcels of not more than one hundred acres for forestry or wildlife purposes and could sell, exchange, or dedicate for recreational purposes all detached parcels under ten acres. This proposal passed the legislature in 1956, but after another year of study and a series of public hearings around the state, the committee abandoned this amendment in favor of the second proposal. This second amendment provided for the sale, exchange, or dedication to other uses of all detached parcels of not more than ten contiguous acres. This amendment passed the legislature in 1956 and 1957 and was presented to the voters in the 1957 general election, when it was approved by a vote of 1,551,982 to 972,118. A later amendment in 1972, approved at the 1973 general election, would raise the acreage limitation from ten acres to one hundred acres (but legislation to implement that increase would not be enacted until Chapter 455 of the Laws of 1976 was approved). The first sale of a detached parcel of forest preserve by the state under this program was in the Catskills, where a 0.517-acre parcel near the City of Kingston was sold in 1960 for $5,725. The law requires that the monies received from the sale of any detached parcel of forest preserve be deposited in a so-called "Forest Preserve Expansion Fund," which must "be expended only for the acquisition of additional lands for such forest preserve within either such Adirondack or Catskill park."

While the detached-parcel question received the major focus, the Committee on Natural Resources and its Special Advisory Committee on the Forest Preserve also considered the "blue lines" and concluded that both park boundaries should be extended "to include all true wilderness areas of both the Adirondack and Catskill Mountain ranges." As might be expected, the Adirondack boundary got the attention, and the committee introduced legislation that was enacted to extend the Adirondack blue line in 1956. It seemed as if the Catskill blue line was not going to be changed. At a public hearing on the detached forest preserve parcel issue, the Catskill Park boundary came up for discussion. Advocates for extending the blue line felt that "one-half of the mountain area of the Catskill region lies outside the Catskill Park, and that seven mountains ranging in elevation from 3,213 feet to 3,598 feet lie north and west of the present Catskill Park." Some of this testimony may have stretched the facts a bit, but the point was made. The committee decided to take another and more detailed look at the Catskill Park boundary.

In the meantime, the Conservation Department was already doing just that. It had asked its three district foresters from the Catskills (one each from Catskill, Middletown, and Oneonta) and the chief of its Catskills land survey crew, to get together and come up with proposals for extending the Catskill Park blue line. This "committee" came up with a number of recommendations. In no special order it suggested that:

1. "All of Great Lot 4 (of the Hardenburgh Patent in Sullivan County) should be included." The existing park boundary at the time was along the northerly line of Great Lot 4. This proposed addition would have brought the remainder of the Town of Rockland, nearly all of the remainder of the Town of Neversink, and a portion of the Town of Liberty into the park.

2. "The large area in the southeast corner of Delaware County bounded south and west by the Delaware River and north by the present blue line should be included." This would have brought a major part of the Town of Hancock and an additional part of the Town of Colchester into the park. It would have extended the park in Delaware County to the Delaware River at the state line with Pennsylvania.

3. "The area including the Binnewater Class of the Kingston Commons and the Ashokan Reservoir area should be included. We feel that the easterly boundary should run along the Esopus Creek and the Thruway to the Town of Saugerties line." This

Served directly by passenger rail, the Simpson Ski Slope near Phoenicia, shown here in the 1930s or 1940s, was the first downhill ski area in New York. (Collection of Lonnie and Peg Gale)

would have added the rest of the Town of Olive, most of the Town of Hurley, the remainder of the Town of Woodstock, all of the Town of Kingston, part of the Town of Ulster, and an additional part of the Town of Wawarsing to the park.

4. "Near Palenville the present line follows up the Cauterskill to North Lake and thence northerly along the top of the mountain and down the Cairo-Catskill town line. We feel that it should cut across from Palenville along the easterly line of the state land tract." This would have added an additional part of the Town of Catskill and brought the blue line to the foot of the eastern escarpment of the Catskill Mountains.

5. The committee was unsure as to whether or not the Town of Halcott should be added. The answer hinged on the possible future status of an existing five-hundred-acre parcel of forest preserve in the town. If that parcel could be managed as a reforestation area, Halcott should be left out of the park. "On the other hand if it is to remain as Forest Preserve, we are of the opinion that all of the Town of Halcott should be brought inside." In the event of the second option, the committee felt an additional part of the Town of Middletown and the remainder of the Town of Lexington should also be included in the expansion.

The extensions proposed to the south and southwest of the existing park were far-reaching. The director of the Division of Lands and Forests reduced these by about half for the Sullivan County portion so as not to include the resort area of that part of the county, and by about 80 percent for the Delaware County portion. The 500-acre parcel in Halcott would always be forest preserve, as best as anyone could foretell, but the expansion proposed here was reduced also. The other proposals were accepted as presented. The director, in passing his recommendations on to the commissioner, said, "There are certain groups who feel that the proposal to sell small detached parcels outside the existing blue line might be extended to include large areas, and I am sure that extension of the blue line as indicated on the maps would overcome some of these objections." So it was that the question of detached parcels would influence the one expansion of the Catskill Park, as it had the creation of the park in the first place.

In the latter part of 1956, the director met with and reported to the Joint Legislative Committee a number of times and worked out a final proposed description for a new Catskill blue line. The final boundary description was introduced by Senator Wheeler Milmoe and Assemblyman Robert Watson Pomeroy, chairman and member, respectively, of the Joint Legislative Committee. The proposal was enacted as Chapter 787 of the Laws of 1957. Unlike when the Catskill Park was first created in 1904, the legislation for the park's one expansion in 1957 gave the park more meaning and substance. A total of 107,660 acres was added to the area of the park, bringing about 8,000 acres of existing forest preserve into the park. In approving the law, Governor Averell Harriman said the purpose of the expansion was "to include areas of forest and recreational value ... and approximately 8,000 acres of Forest Preserve, some of which are of substantial size and properly belong within the confines of the park." He went on to say, "This is part of the ten-point conservation program which I announced last year and which included enlargement of the forest preserve." This shows that even governors don't understand the difference between the park and the forest preserve.

Again not much was said, officially or otherwise, about the Catskill Park and its new blue line. One has to search closely through the 1957 annual report of the Conservation Department to find any discussion of it at all. Only one reference appears, and that is in a notation at the bottom of the tables usually included to give the county-by-county acreage of the forest preserve lands inside and outside of the two park boundaries. This notation says, simply, "The above acreage figures inside and outside

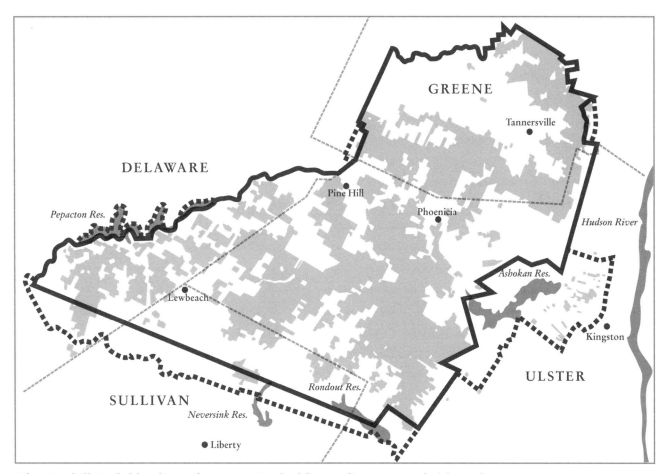

The Catskill Park blue line, after 1957. Dashed line indicates extended boundaries. Shaded areas indicate forest preserve as of 1982. (Adapted from map in NYSDEC Collection)

the blue line have been adjusted to conform to recent changes in the … Catskill Park boundary." An examination of these acreage figures shows that something was amiss with the 8,000 acres of pre-existing forest preserve first stated by the department, and repeated by the governor, to have been inscribed within the new park boundary. The "Outside Blue Line" acreage for Delaware County was listed as being reduced by 313 acres to a new total of 3,993.25 acres; the Greene County figures had been reduced by 109.16 acres to 1,347.02 acres; Sullivan County had been reduced by 343.25 acres to 938.33 acres; and the "Outside Blue Line" acreage for Ulster County had been reduced by 3,731.93 acres to a new total of 1,731.22 acres. In all, the acreage of previously detached forest preserve that had now been brought inside the Catskill Park was 4,497.7 acres, which is far less than the originally reported total of 8,009.82 acres. No issue seems to have been raised by anyone about the 3,500-acre difference between the first and second reported figures, which is perhaps why so little was said about the new Catskill Park in the annual report.

In the end the blue line had been expanded in seven areas: 1) in Sullivan County the new line went through the middle of Great Lot 4, following lot lines and the Willowemoc and Beaverkill rivers, to include additional parts of the Towns of Neversink and Rockland; 2) in Delaware County the boundary continued along the Beaverkill and the southwesterly line of the Town of Colchester to include an additional part of that town; 3) also in Delaware County, the line was moved from the southeasterly bank of the East Branch Delaware River to the northwesterly bank, to include the Pepacton Reservoir, a part of the Town of Hancock, and additional parts of the towns of Colchester, Andes, and Middletown; 4) in western Greene County the blue line was moved west to include a part of the Town of Halcott; 5) in northeastern Greene County it was moved to the foot of the eastern Catskill escarpment, as had been suggested by the departmental committee, to include an additional part of the Town of Catskill; 6) in eastern Ulster County it also followed the recommendation of the committee and moved the park boundary east to include the Ashokan Reservoir, the remainder of the towns of Olive and Woodstock, all of the Town of Kingston, and parts of the towns of Hurley and Ulster; and 7) in southern Ulster County, it was moved south to include the remainder of the Rondout Reservoir and an additional part of the Town of Wawarsing, again as the committee had recommended.

A comprehensive survey of the state's outdoor recreational resources was ordered by Governor Nelson Rockefeller in 1959. The state Conservation Department welcomed the opportunity to demonstrate and document the pressing need for more land and more recreational facilities across the state. The survey was completed quickly and a report was submitted to the governor in February 1960. It noted the population increase of the state as well as an increase in personal income and leisure time. It emphasized the growing popularity of outdoor recreation and the department's inability to keep pace with the needs and demands of the public because of insufficient lands and recreational improvements. The report explicitly called attention to the deficiency of land for campsites, parks, public fishing access, boat launches, multiple use needs, participant sports, and wetlands protection and called for better consolidation and access for the forest preserve. Particular note was made of the fast rate at which open land was being used for residential purposes and other uses contrary to public recreation. The title of the report was *Now or Never*, and what that meant was perfectly clear. The report

recommended that a bond issue of $75 million be put before the people of the state. Governor Rockefeller went before the 1960 state legislature and urged it to consider the recommendations, noting that it was a fitting measure on the year of the seventy-fifth anniversary of the state forest preserve.

The legislature was not long in acting, and in April 1960 three laws were passed: Chapter 522 authorized the creation of a $75 million state debt to "provide monies to acquire predominantly open or natural lands for conservation and outdoor recreation"; Chapter 523 set up procedures to implement the bond act and allocate funds for specific purposes; and Chapter 759 specifically addressed new provisions and procedures for

The old way of life in the Catskill Mountains, early 1900s. (Collection of Town of Neversink)

acquiring or appropriating forest preserve land. The voters of the state favored the bond act and it passed in November 1960 with a vote of 2,390,585 to 889,284. Of the overall funds, $2.9 million was reserved for purchases of additional forest preserve lands and $4.9 million was allocated for purchasing lands for campgrounds, some of which would be in the forest preserve counties. The department quickly began acquisition work in early 1961, and the category under which forest preserve lands were acquired was called Wilderness Consolidation and Access. This title was chosen in anticipation of possible legislation resulting from a study of wilderness area designations by the Joint Legislative Committee on Natural Resources.

Acquisitions proceeded steadily under the 1960 bond act; however, it was quickly realized that the overall sum of money was not going to be enough to achieve the goals outlined in the original report on the recreational needs of the state. Appraisals made for actual purchases clearly indicated that the

Hay farmers in East Jewett, circa 1910. (Collection of Larry Tompkins)

estimated prices had been too low, and the department recommended additional funding in 1962. A new bond issue for an additional $25 million was enacted by the legislature and approved by a vote of the people, 1,786,496 to 889,924. The number of votes against this second bond issue was almost the same as the number against the first—the same opposition voters who went to the polls in 1960 must have gone again in 1962. Of the second round of money, only $100,000 was available for forest preserve purchases, and the department applied it mostly to increasing access in remote wilderness areas. It was not until 1971 that the funds provided by the 1960 and 1962 bond acts were finally expended. In the Catskills, sixty-six parcels were purchased, totaling more than twelve thousand acres, for a total of $451,000. The average price of $37.10 per acre in the Catskills in the 1960s was not all that much higher than the $9.59 per acre paid for lands acquired under the 1924 bond issue.

The various park regions of the state were redefined by Chapter 665 of the Laws of 1967. As previously, the Council of Parks and Outdoor Recreation (now the New York State Office of Parks, Recreation, and Historic Preservation [OPRHP]) was responsible for outdoor recreational programs and facilities in five regions covering most of the state, while the Conservation Department remained responsible for recreational programs and facilities within the sixth park region, comprising the Adirondacks and Catskills. Heretofore, the "sixth park region" had been defined as being the entire of the four Catskill and the twelve Adirondack counties, but the 1967 law defined the sixth region as being those parts of these counties "lying within the Adirondack or Catskill parks."

In 1967 there was also another Constitutional Convention. In regard to the forest preserve, there were several proposals made for increased management and human improvements, some of which would have legalized things that were already being done. One proposal suggested that certain areas along highways be zoned for intensive recreation. Another proposal suggested cutting timber on parts of the preserve for the purposes of silviculture (forest management and timber harvesting) and forestry research. Another proposal recommended that wildlife habitat improvement projects be allowed on parts of the preserve. Other proposals called for: the establishment of different management zones in the preserve; redefining the forest preserve to include only those state lands inside the blue lines; and even redefining the forest preserve to include only those lands inside wilderness areas. As stated earlier, these measures did not pass.

A new state campground was added to the Catskill Park in 1967—the Mongaup Pond Campground in the Town of Rockland. The Little Pond Campground was added a year later, straddling the towns of Andes and Hardenburgh. Chapter 1052 of the Laws of 1969 brought outdoor advertising sign controls to the Catskill Park, again following the lead of the Adirondacks, where such controls were implemented in 1924. The purpose of such controls, according to the law, is "to con-

serve the natural beauty of the Adirondack and Catskill parks, to preserve and regulate the said parks for public uses for the resort of the public for recreation, pleasure, air, light and enjoyment, to keep them open, safe, clean, and in good order for the welfare of society, and to protect and conserve the investment of the state in forest lands, campsites and other interests in real property in said parks." The sign law is designed to limit the location, number, size, and appearance of signs that are located on private land, but off the premises of the advertising business. It stands as the only land use control imposed on private land attributable to the Catskill Park designation.

As the 1960s passed and the decade of the 1970s began, so also began a new era for the Conservation Department. After over a century of a succession of government agencies concerned with natural resources, and thus the environment, the State of New York suddenly "discovered" the environment and created the New York State Department of Environmental Conservation (NYSDEC). The new agency subsumed the responsibilities of the old Conservation Department as well as parts of the Department of Health and various other commissions and boards, and took effect on July 1, 1970. Another major development that took place at this time was the creation of the Adirondack Park Agency in 1971. The two state agencies quickly worked together to develop a master plan for classifying and managing the Adirondack forest preserve lands, and the Adirondack Park State Land Master Plan was adopted in 1972.

Also in 1971, at the prompting of a young, private, nonprofit organization, The Catskill Center for Conservation and Development (founded in 1969), the legislature created a Temporary State Commission to Study the Catskills, similar to a commission that had begun studying the Adirondack region a few years earlier. The ten-member volunteer commission was comprised of Kirby Peake (chairman of the Catskill Commission) of Bronxville; Mitchell Brock (vice chairman) of New York City and Claryville; Harold Finkle (secretary) of Kingston; Robert Bishop of DeLancey; Jerome Ehrlich of South Fallsburg; Scott E. Greene of Cooperstown and Roxbury; Melvin Lynes of Middleburg; Helen Potter of Newburgh; Roswell Sanford of Margaretville; and Israel Slutzky of Hunter. The commission was assisted in its work by a paid professional staff.

Additionally, a ten-member staff team, or "Catskill Task Force," from NYSDEC was appointed to aid the Temporary State Commission to Study the Catskills by conducting several of the associated studies, especially those relating to state land, natural resources, and fish and wildlife in the Catskills. The NYSDEC team was appointed by Commissioner Peter A. A. Berle, and included Theodore L. Hullar, deputy commissioner for Programs and Research (chairman of the NYSDEC staff team); Thomas P. Eichler, director of the Office of Program Development, Planning, and Research (OPDPR); John A. Finck, assistant director for Plan Development, OPDPR; James O. Preston, director of the Division of Lands and Forests; Herbert E. Doig, director of the Division of Fish and Wildlife; Holt Bodinson, director of the Division of Educational Services; Terence P. Curran, director of the Office of Environmental Analysis; Athan A. Baskous, director of the Region 4 Office; Norman J. Van Valkenburgh, director of the Region 3 Office; Warren McKeon, former director of the Region 3 Office; and Charles C. Morrison Jr., chief of Land Resources Planning, OPDPR.

The Catskill commission was asked by the state legislature to provide recommendations "for the improvement of the general quality of life in the Catskill Region." The geographic extent of the region under consideration was far-reaching (originally including all of eight counties, including Chenango County), but it was centered around the four counties containing the Catskill Park. Although this commission, before it went out of existence in 1976, did not focus solely on the Catskill Park and forest preserve, some of its recommendations did. For one thing, it felt that the detached forest preserve parcels over one hundred acres should be either dedicated to other forestry or wildlife purposes or exchanged for land inside the Catskill Park, and the commission proposed an amendment to the constitution to allow that to happen. It recommended that emphasis be given to acquisition of additional lands inside the park to provide improved access to existing forest preserve. The commission also recommended that the lands of the forest preserve inside the Catskill Park be classified according to their characteristics and capacity to withstand public use, and specifically urged that four wilderness areas be established (these being the same four areas identified as suitable wilderness areas by the Joint Legislative Committee on Natural Resources in 1961).

At about the same time the commission's reports were being issued, The Catskill Center for Conservation and Development issued reports based on its own studies and perceptions. The Catskill Center agreed with and repeated the recommendation for four wilderness areas. Similarly, it agreed that the forest preserve inside the Catskill Park should be classified (in addition to the wilderness areas) according to their capacity to withstand recreational use. In a major departure, however, The Catskill Center said that some of the state lands should be classified to other than forest preserve purposes and there was a need to "consider seriously the multiple use and dominant use management potential of portions of" these lands.

With regard to the Catskill Park boundary, or blue line, The Catskill Center made specific recommendations for changes in two locations. First of all, it urged that the blue line be extended in the northwest corner of the park so as to include the remainder of the towns of Halcott and Lexington. The reasoning for this paralleled that of the department committee when it looked at the same area in 1956. The proposed 14,270-acre expansion would include the one 500-acre forest preserve parcel in the Town of Halcott and bring the remaining two peaks over 3,500 feet in elevation—Bearpen and Vly

Sawing ice on Colgate Lake, date unknown. (Collection of Larry Tompkins)

mountains—into the park. The Catskill Center wanted to reduce the park area in the vicinity of the City of Kingston and then rededicate "the scattered and isolated parcels [of forest preserve] in the vicinity of Stony Hollow for a variety of more intensive recreation uses." The recommendations of the commission and The Catskill Center were not implemented, although in the late 1970s the department did prepare a draft master plan for the state land inside the Catskill Park. This plan did set out the four wilderness areas and classified the remaining state lands in less restrictive categories within the constraints of the provisions of the state constitution.

No question seems to have been raised over the years concerning the size of the Catskill Park. The figure of 576,120 acres as first stated by the 1905 Forest, Fish, and Game Commission for the size of the original park is generally accepted. Also accepted is the 107,660-acre figure issued by the Conservation Department in 1957 as an addition to the park. In the same year, however, the department said the total area of the park was 657,600 acres. Adding the 1957 expansion acreage to the original acreage totals 683,780 acres, or 26,180 acres more than the official stated acreage. To add

further confusion, the Joint Legislative Committee on Natural Resources seemed to have forgotten it had brought about the 1957 expansion by stating in its 1961 report that the Catskill Park "contains 576,000 acres of which 227,000 are state-owned Forest Preserve lands and 349,000 acres are privately owned." If anyone noticed the discrepancies, nothing was done about it.

The opportunity to straighten this out came in early 1982 when another state agency asked the Real Property unit in the NYSDEC's Region 4 Office (in Schenectady) for the area of each of the four Catskill counties within the Catskill Park. By that time the Catskill land map had run through a number of editions, but the latest (prepared in 1970) had resulted from a complete redrafting effort using the new United States Geological Survey 7.5° quadrangles as base

Loading blocks of ice cut from Colgate Lake, date unknown. (Collection of Larry Tompkins)

maps. Using the more accurate mapping, it soon became obvious to the land surveyors that an even greater error existed than previously thought. So they started at the beginning and calculated the original acreage, plus the 1957 expansion acreage, finally determining the official park area still recognized today.

The original land surveyors knew their business. The 1904 Catskill Park, as determined by the new survey, included a total of 577,200 acres, only about 1,000 acres different from what had been first estimated. It was during the 1957 expansion that things went amiss. The actual expansion was 128,300 acres, some 20,000 acres different from what had been published at the time. And so the correct acreage of the present-day Catskill Park is 705,500 acres.

In answering the question first posed, the Region 4 land surveyors determined the county acreages inside the Catskill Park to be: 103,860 acres of Delaware County; 168,220 acres of Greene County; 88,375 acres of Sullivan County; and 345,045 acres of Ulster County. Going one step farther, the acreage of the seven areas of the 1957 expansion was determined. The southerly expansion in Sullivan County added 31,930 acres; the addition in the Town of Colchester, Delaware County included 15,100 acres; the Pepacton Reservoir addition in Delaware County included 2,750 acres; the expansion into the Town of Halcott, Greene County added 2,320 acres; the addition in northeasterly Greene County included 4,230 acres; the Ashokan Reservoir area expansion in Ulster County added 64,200 acres; and the Rondout

Reservoir area in southerly Ulster County added 7,770 acres to the park.

In 1972 the people of the state were again presented with a bond act, this time in the amount of $1.15 billion "to preserve and enhance New York's environment." The Environmental Quality Bond Act of 1972 was passed by a vote of 3,060,063 to 1,518,579 and provided a total of $175 million "to preserve priceless land resources," with $59 million earmarked for the Adirondack Park and $15 million for the Catskill Park. Consolidation of forest preserve lands and improved access were again key goals of the NYSDEC in using the land acquisition money. These bond act monies lasted into the late 1980s, overlapping a bit with the next successful environmental bond act in 1986. Some 116 land acquisition projects in the Catskill forest preserve were completed through the 1972 bond act, adding 35,527 acres to the public domain. The average price of land in the Catskills over the decade-and-a-half span of time was just over $400 per acre.

1975 was a banner year for adding lands to the Catskill forest preserve using the new bond act money, with many acquisitions large and small. In that year the state purchased a 1,363-acre tract in Bushnellsville, adding to the Westkill Wilderness; a 636-acre in-holding (private property surrounded, or nearly so, by state land) in the heart of Peekamoose Valley, which included Buttermilk Falls; and a 614-acre parcel that was originally slated for a subdivision, along the Esopus Valley in the Town of Shandaken. The largest acquisition in 1975, however, was the purchase of 1,658 acres in the upper East Kill Valley in the towns of Jewett and Hunter, from the Robert Colgate estate for $475,000. The property extended from mountain ridge to mountain ridge across the valley—all forested except for a 200-acre clearing with some buildings—and the 25-acre Colgate Lake. The acquisition effectively surrounded with state land another 4,363-acre property further up the valley that was also being sold by the Colgate estate. The state was interested in acquiring that land as well; however, the Boy's Club of New York City offered a higher price. Patience paid off, and in 1979 the property came on the market again. Negotiations were long and difficult, but in the fall of 1980 a total of 4,163 acres were added to the Catskill forest preserve at a cost of $1,256,000, with the remaining 200 acres, including a 45-acre lake, sold to the New York State Office of Mental Retardation and Development Disabilities.

Another major conservation project using the 1972 bond act funds brought several thousand acres of wilderness in the Beaverkill River headwaters into the forest preserve. On April 22, 1976, The Catskill Center for Conservation and Development received its largest gift of land ever—approximately 3,600 acres of wild forest land in the Town of Hardenburgh from the members of the Balsam Lake Club. Located in the heart of the Catskill Park, surrounded almost entirely by state forest preserve, the property is located on the western flanks of Graham

and Doubletop mountains, extending along the Beaverkill Valley between the Beaverkill Range and Woodpecker Ridge. Termed the "Beaverkill Conservation Area" at the time, this property represented one of the largest tracts of privately owned forest land in the Catskill Park. The gift of this unique property generated considerable interest, and The Catskill Center's board received both criticism and praise for voting to accept it.

The Balsam Lake Club, established in the 1880s, is one of the oldest fly-fishing clubs in the country. Over the years the club acquired old farmsteads, and by the 1970s it had amassed over 3,600 acres. Despite their commitment to preserving the land in its natural state, members began to question their ability to keep the club going when taxes began to soar in the early 1970s. By 1975 the club had fallen into arrears and began to consider a number of options, including selling off or perhaps developing a portion of the large tract, or negotiating a sale to New York State. By 1976 the tax bills continued to pile up, but at the time the state was not prepared to act quickly on an acquisition.

The club began to approach organizations dedicated to open space preservation, and it was eventually decided that any gift of club lands should be given to a locally based organization. Negotiations between the club and The Catskill Center resulted in a gift of 3,615 acres of unimproved land, plus a fund to assist with the settlement of back taxes and management of the property. The newly named Balsam Lake Anglers Club and its members retained approximately 145 acres, including Balsam Lake, a strip of land along

The traditional way of gathering maple sap in springtime, early 1900s. (Collection of The Catskill Center)

both sides of the Beaverkill River, and all buildings and other improvements. This portion of the property still remains in the private ownership of the club, and is protected from further development by a conservation easement held by The Catskill Center.

The Catskill Center originally intended to convey to the state for inclusion in the forest preserve some of the property it had accepted, but retain and manage most of the Beaverkill Conservation Area as an education and research preserve. Complete state ownership became inevitable, however, because of a long and expensive legal dispute between The Catskill Center and the Town of Hardenburgh over property tax exemption. During the three years that The Catskill Center owned the property, a detailed natural resource and forest inventory was conducted that formed the basis of a management plan developed in coordination with the NYSDEC. In July 1979, the State of New York acquired the property from The Catskill Center with funds from the 1972 bond act. Proceeds from the sale were used to establish an endowment that continues to help support The Catskill Center's land conservation, community development, and educational work in the region today.

NYSDEC land acquisition staff were very busy during the 1970s and 1980s completing many other notable Catskill forest preserve projects using the 1972 bond act money. The seventh and final state campground in the Catskill Park was established in 1979—Kenneth Wilson State Campground in the Town of Woodstock. Also in that year, the state picked up 576 acres along the upper West Branch Neversink River on both sides of Frost Valley Road from the Shandaken Rod and Gun Club. A year later the land next to this was purchased from the Winnisook Club. The 803-acre acquisition was split in two pieces, with one piece giving much better public access to the trail to Slide Mountain, and the other piece encompassing the trail to Giant Ledge—two of the most popular hiking destinations in the Catskill Mountains. Another highly significant purchase in 1980 was of the former Alder Lake Boy Scout Camp, with a total of 1,610 acres that included the beautiful 45-acre Alder Lake and the historic Coykendall Mansion overlooking it. Acquisitions in the mid to late 1980s (but still using 1972 bond act money) included 1,880 acres across the east face of Mount Pleasant in the Town of

Shandaken, overlooking the Route 28 corridor; 964 acres on the west side of Oliverea Valley in the Town of Shandaken, along the Esopus tributary known as the Elk Bushkill; 756 acres on the back side of Hanover Mountain, between Maltby Hollow and Watson Hollow in the Town of Olive; 615 acres around Huggins Lake, with a dirt access road from Berry Brook Road, in the Town of Colchester; and 595 acres on Sheridan Mountain, to the west of Route 214 in Chichester, in the Town of Shandaken. Just west of Hodge and Frick ponds in the Sullivan County town of Rockland, the state purchased in 1987 no less than 2,179 acres from a private landowner named Neil Brown. The ponds themselves, and the land connecting them to this earlier purchase, were picked up two years later in an acquisition funded under the 1986 bond act.

Maple sap-collecting buckets, early 1900s. (Collection of Delaware County Historical Association)

Land acquisition initiatives that focus on expanding a particular unit of state land with the goal of making it more contiguous can go on for decades. This fact may best be illustrated by the example of North-South Lake Campground. As with any public facility, especially one as popular as North-South Lake Campground, there becomes a need for additional land and expanded capacity as time goes by and public use increases. When the North Lake Campsite was developed for public camping use in 1930, it had "one half mile of gravel road, fifteen fireplaces, twenty tables and benches, two improved chemical latrines, standard ranger headquarters, and the installation of temporary water supply." In addition to the initial 2,197-acre parcel acquired in 1930, another 619 acres were acquired (for $6,196) the same year, this piece lying south of the outlet stream of the lake and extending to Route 23A. Three years later a 252-acre parcel adjoining the last acquisition to the east was also acquired, for $10 per acre.

The next piece was not obtained until nearly three decades later, when in 1961 ten acres just east of North Lake were taken from The Nature Conservancy through the process of condemnation for $25,100. The story behind this acquisition is an interesting one. The ten acres had been parted off from the Catskill Mountain House property in 1953 for the development of a tourist attraction known as "Rip's Retreat" where old Rip Van Winkle would wander around with his dog, and gnomes would treat visitors to

glass-blowing and wooden shoe-making demonstrations. In the ensuing years, however, interest in Rip waned and business was suffering. The owner failed to make mortgage payments on the property, and the Federal Small Business Administration put the property up for auction. The department was prevented by law from purchasing the property by bid at auction, so at the last minute a representative of The Nature Conservancy from Washington D.C. was engaged to attend the auction to try to acquire the land. The Nature Conservancy was successful in purchasing the property for $25,000. An extra $100 was paid to The Nature Conservancy when the state subsequently took over the property to cover the bidder's plane ticket.

Additions to the North Lake Campsite continued in May 1962 when another 259 acres were acquired for $61,000. This was the last of the Catskill Mountain House property and contained the crumbling relic of that once imposing and world-famous hotel. The remains of the hotel were burned by the NYSDEC the following January. A second condemnation proceeding in 1962 added another 275 acres to the campground, including the entirety of South Lake. The appropriation was filed against Carpathian Vacation Camp Inc.; however, it turned out to involve more than thirty separate lot owners. Claims were filed for over $2 million, but when finally settled, the total of all payments came to $545,500. The final 57-acre parcel was purchased in 1975 from Columbia University for $31,500. This last piece was located just south of the former site of the Catskill Mountain

House and brought virtually the entire north-eastern Catskill Mountain escarpment under state ownership.

In 1986 the people of New York once again spoke out in favor of the environment, passing another environmental-quality bond act for $1.45 billion. The vote was 1,524,550 for and 745,554 against. The bulk of this money, $1.2 billion, was to be used to clean up hazardous waste sites, with the balance to be used for other purposes such as land acquisition. In the Catskill Park, only twenty-one fee acquisitions totaling 3,460 acres and three conservation easements totaling 514 acres are attributed to the 1986 bond act money. The total amount expended for the fee and easement purchases was $4,281,584. The largest project from this funding source was the acquisition of three parcels totaling 1,738 acres from the Open Space Institute (OSI) in 1989. This land encompassed Quick Lake and Frick Pond in the Town of Rockland and added substantially to the Willowemoc Wild Forest. The state also purchased a conservation easement from OSI on a neighboring 287-acre parcel containing Hodge Pond, and OSI maintains this property today as the Beech Mountain Nature Preserve. Other notable state land acquisition projects in the Catskills using 1986 bond act money include 612 acres purchased on Plateau Mountain, 530 acres in Mink Hollow, 384 acres on the northern side of Halcott Mountain, and 313 acres on Overlook Mountain.

In 1990 New York Governor Mario Cuomo and the state legislature authorized the development of the state's first statewide land conservation prioritization plan. The first New York State Open Space Plan was completed in 1992 with the assistance and input of nine regional advisory committees (one per each NYSDEC region). Regional advisory committees include representatives of counties and municipalities as well as professionals in the fields of land conservation, historic preservation, planning, outdoor recreation, and other related interest areas. The state's Open Space Plan is updated every three years and provides priority area and policy recommendations for guiding the land conservation activities of the NYSDEC and OPRHP. The 1992 plan identified the forest preserve as a major resource category and called for a new, dedicated funding source for implementing the plan's recommendations.

In 1993 the state passed the Environmental Protection Act, which set forth a dedicated Environmental Protection Fund (EPF) to be used annually for a variety of land conservation and environmental improvement projects around the state. The New York State Open Space Plan describes the EPF as a permanently dedicated funding source that is derived primarily from revenues stemming from a portion of the proceeds of a state real estate transfer tax, refinancing of state and public authority obligations, sale of surplus state lands as authorized by state law, sale or lease of state-owned underwater lands, and sales of special license plates designed to raise funds for open space conservation. In the Catskills, sizable acquisitions that have been made by the state using EPF funds include 610 acres on Plateau Mountain in 1997; 1,189 acres on Bearpen Mountain just outside the Catskill Park (managed as state forest) in 1999; a 160-acre parcel in Peck Hollow in 2000 that comprised half of an in-holding surrounded by the West Kill Wilderness Area; and then the other half of the Peck Hollow in-holding, just recently in 2003, which added another 187 acres to the wilderness area.

In 1996 a new state bond act, known as the Clean Water/Clean Air Bond Act, was passed under the leadership of Governor George Pataki. The bond act provided $1.75 billion for land conservation, environmental protection and remediation, land steward-ship, air and water quality improvement, recreational improvements, and other envi-ronmental projects. This ballot measure passed by a public vote of 2,084,658 to 1,637,272. All of the funds for land acquisi-tion under the 1996 bond act were either expended or fully committed to pending projects by 2002. In 2000 an acquisition proj-ect under this bond act brought 412 acres along the Willowemoc Creek corridor into the Catskill forest preserve, and an addition-al 500 acres added to the Bearpen State Forest (state forest outside the park) in 2001. The most notable 1996 bond act acquisition in the Catskills, with partial funding from the EPF, was the purchase of 4,789 acres of the former Lundy estate, as well as an associated conser-vation easement on 462 acres, from the Open Space Institute and the Trust for Public Land (TPL) in 2002. This land, located in the Ulster County towns of Rochester and

Huckleberry and blueberry pickers in Chichester, circa 1900. (Collection of Lonnie and Peg Gale)

Wawarsing, lies partially within and partially outside of the Catskill Park boundary. That portion outside of the park, approximately 3,700 acres, will be managed as the new Vernooy Kill State Forest, and the remaining portion lying inside the park is classified as forest preserve and will be managed as part of the Sundown Wild Forest. The whole parcel encompasses six miles of the Vernooy Kill Creek, a noted trout stream and the largest undammed tributary of the Rondout Creek.

As alluded to in some of these project descriptions, the state often gets assistance from nonprofit land conservation organizations in increasing its public land holdings. In addition to some of the large Catskills tracts noted above, there are other important places where forest preserve lands were protected with the help of land trusts. The Catskill Center for Conservation and Development helped acquire and convey to NYSDEC the 104-acre Fawn's Leap waterfall parcel in the heart of Kaaterskill Clove in 1995. In 1999 the state accepted a gift of 308 acres on Mongaup Mountain from the Open Space Institute. The Woodstock Land Conservancy and the Open Space Institute also partnered last year (2003) to acquire two critical parcels totaling 291 acres on Overlook Mountain, and are working to acquire additional lands to add to the Overlook Mountain Wild Forest. The Open Space Institute also recently purchased 259 acres on the Willowemoc Creek on behalf of the state, and OSI and the NYSDEC celebrated this acquisition with a press event on the opening day of trout season this year (April 1, 2004). The property is the former Van Norden estate once owned

by the Willowemoc Club, one of the first private fly-fishing clubs in the Catskills (and in the nation), founded in 1869. This property will now offer its excellent fishing opportunities to the public. Also in this centennial year of the Catskill Park, The Catskill Center has transferred two parcels of land amounting to forty-one acres at the head of Kaaterskill Clove into state ownership. The opening of the new Nature Conservancy office in the Catskill Mountains in April 2003 is likely to greatly increase this type of nonprofit land conservation assistance in the Catskill region for years to come.

Negotiations around regulations and land use issues pertaining to the New York City Watershed area of the Catskill Mountains were facilitated by Governor Pataki's office in the mid-1990s, and culminated in a landmark Memorandum of Agreement (MOA) between New York City, New York State, towns in the New York City Watershed area, and various environmental groups in 1997. One of the outcomes of the MOA was the initiation of an ambitious land and conservation easement acquisition program to be implemented by the New York City Department of Environmental Protection (NYCDEP). The goal of the program is to limit development and protect important wetlands, floodplains, stream corridors, and forested and agricultural lands in an effort to maintain good water quality in the Catskill/Delaware water supply system. The city's Land Acquisition

Program has been quite successful in acquiring land and conservation easements throughout the watershed during the first seven years of the initiative. As of June 2004, the NYCDEP had acquired, or was in the process of acquiring, nearly 35,000 acres of land in fee, plus over 6,000 acres under conservation easement in the West-of-Hudson Catskill/Delaware Watershed area (with more land and easements in the East-of-Hudson Watershed area). Add to this the approximately 34,000 acres of reservoir buffer land around the six Catskill/Delaware reservoirs that New York City owned prior to the MOA and approximately 8,000 acres of active farmland in the Catskill/Delaware Watershed that is currently protected, or is in the process of being protected, by conservation easements held by the Watershed Agricultural Council.

The area of overlap between the New York City Watershed and the Catskill Park encompasses approximately 455,160 acres, with approximately 65 percent of the Catskill Park being within the NYC Watershed, and approximately 45 percent of the NYC Watershed being within the Catskill Park. There are now approximately 30,000 acres of New York City-owned and protected land within the Catskill Park, and conversely there are approximately 188,000 acres of Catskill forest preserve within the NYC Watershed boundary. In this overlapping area, the state forest preserve lands and the NYC Watershed lands generally complement each other and have compatible purposes. Ever since the first of New York City's Catskill region water sup-

ply reservoirs began collecting water in 1915 (the Ashokan Reservoir), the mountainous forest preserve has been pivotal to the production and protection of clean drinking water for millions of people. Similar in its multiple conservation values, the lands owned by NYCDEP also protect important wildlife habitat, contribute to the scenic draw of the region, and add to the outdoor recreational opportunities available in the region in addition to maintaining good water quality. Many of the newly acquired city lands border forest preserve lands, thereby adding to the contiguous base of protected land and offering new public access points.

The Catskill Park and forest preserve received renewed attention in the late 1990s when the state authorized a study to be conducted by a team of work groups and stakeholders. Their goal was to assess the opportunities and challenges associated with

Mountains and meadow in Shady. (Chris Olney)

public awareness and public access to the Catskill Park and forest preserve and make recommendations for improvements. The Catskill Forest Preserve Public Access Plan was released in August 1999; it provides an overview of the public use of the Catskill Park and forest preserve, highlights both shortcomings and successes, proposes a much-needed vision for improving and enhancing public awareness of and access to this great resource, and provides specific action steps for realizing that vision. It is a well-written and forward-thinking blueprint for making the Catskill Park and forest preserve a more integrated part of the Catskill region and its communities. The key issues addressed by the Public Access Plan include: enhancement of scenic travel corridors; better distribution of information and public outreach through brochures, maps, kiosks, Web sites, interpretive programs, etc.; improvement of trails and other recreational features; improved access for people with disabilities; improvement of links between the forest preserve and private lands and communities; and better visitor management. The Catskill Forest Preserve Public Access Plan is certainly a document that is intended to address many of the Catskill Park's most pressing needs and to help guide the park into the future.

Perhaps the origin and evolution of the Catskill Park is not quite as mysterious as it seems. The reasons for the Catskill Park and forest preserve coming into being are quite distinct from those behind the beginnings of the Adirondack Park and forest preserve, but each has grown and evolved on similar tracks and both have come to enjoy a special place in the hearts of New Yorkers. The Catskill Park certainly stands today as an invaluable asset to the people of the state and beyond.

Land Management

Public Lands

Given that the Catskill forest preserve is constitutionally protected as a collection of "forever wild" natural areas, with no timber harvesting or deliberate habitat alteration allowed, one might assume that there would be no need for any kind of management or stewardship of those lands once they are acquired—that they simply need to be left alone while nature is allowed to take her course. Certainly one of the primary reasons for protecting the most mountainous lands in the state as forest preserve is to safeguard natural ecosystems and preserve whole landscapes where resources are not extracted and natural cycles may continue without interruption or disturbance. The forest preserve exists not only for the benefit of nature, however, but also for the benefit of people. The citizens of the state, who collectively own the forest preserve, demand access to these lands for outdoor recreation, nature study, and personal enjoyment and reflection.

There has been a long history of outdoor recreation in the Catskills. Long before the forest preserve was established, the mountains were filled with people who loved to fill their lungs with clean mountain air as they stretched their legs among the streams and forests. The great trout streams of the Catskills have always attracted fishermen from New York City and elsewhere, and for centuries people have turned to the hills for hunting game in the fall. Walking among the scenic areas of the mountains was a favorite pastime of the upscale clientele who stayed at the famous and numerous Catskill Mountain hotels during their heyday in the late 1800s and early 1900s. After the forest preserve was created, the Catskills became home to the first hiking trail commissioned by the state (authorized in 1892), leading to the summit of the Catskills' tallest peak—Slide Mountain. As the acreage of the forest preserve increased over the years, and as the recovering and regenerating forests began to mature, the building of public trails and lean-tos also increased, as did the recreational use of these public lands. Hiking and outdoor clubs such as the Appalachian Mountain Club, the NY/NJ Trail Conference, and the Adirondack Mountain Club came to the Catskills more and more for recreation, and the Catskill 3500 Club formed to recognize those people who ventured to all of the highest peaks in the region. Today there are over three hundred miles of marked foot trails in the Catskill Park, and these clubs often work with the state land managers on trail maintenance projects and help make the Catskills a great place to hike and camp.

So, who determines what activities, recreational or otherwise, are allowed on forest preserve lands? Who determines which, how many, and where, human "improvements" such as hiking trails, horse trails, snowmobile trails, footbridges, kiosks, lean-tos, parking areas, campgrounds, and even ski areas might be allowed and built on forest preserve land to accommodate the public demand for recreational access and opportunity? The responsibility for the care and management of the Catskill forest preserve, including decisions on what structures and other improvements may or may not be allowed, lies with NYSDEC. Their management decisions are always a balancing act between resource protection and public access. Forest preserve management is constrained and directed by multiple documents, including the New York State Constitution, New York State Environmental Conservation Law, the Catskill Park State Land Master Plan, and individual unit management plans written for specific land areas.

🌿 🌿 🌿

Article XIV, Section 1, of the New York State Constitution provides the basic "forever wild" protection for our cherished forest preserve lands, and reads simply: "The lands of the State, now owned or hereafter acquired, constituting the forest preserve as now fixed by law, shall be forever kept as wild forest lands. They shall not be leased, sold or exchanged, or be taken by any corporation, public or private, nor shall the timber thereon be sold, removed or destroyed." Since 1894 these two sentences have remained the basic principle from which all decisions relating to the forest preserve have been based, subject to the legal, administrative, and popular interpretations of succeeding generations. Changes to the New York State Constitution can only occur when passed by two consecutive sessions of the state legislature and a subsequent public referendum. According to the Catskill Forest Preserve Public Access Plan (released in August 1999), over two thousand amendments to Article XIV have been introduced in the legislature since 1895, with just twenty-nine actually presented to the people of the state for a vote. Only twenty have been approved and passed into law. Past amendments to Article XIV have addressed some of the management and land exchange issues specific to certain areas of the Adirondack

Barn-raising in Jewett, 1912. (Collection of Larry Tompkins)

and Catskill forest preserve, such as reservoir and state highway construction on forest preserve lands. Constitutional amendments have even gone so far as to create entire downhill ski centers and their associated facilities and amenities on forest preserve land, in both the Adirondacks and Catskills. The justification for such intensive and large-scale recreational development on "forever wild" land has always been promoted as a way to boost slumping rural economies by meeting a high public demand for this type of recreation.

New York State Environmental Conservation Law also provides statutory guidance for management of New York's forest preserve. Whereas the basic constitutional protection of the forest preserve can be considered stable over time, laws tend to evolve more frequently to accommodate changing circumstances. Early laws pertaining to the forest preserve focused mostly on prevention of forest fires and minimizing rampant resource degradation, whereas many of today's laws focus more on public recreational use of state lands. Section 1-0101 of New York State Environmental Conservation Law (ECL) declares that it is state policy to preserve "the unique qualities of special resources such as the Adirondack and Catskill forest preserves." Section 9-0101 of the ECL defines the Catskill Park to include all those lands (public and private) in the counties of Delaware, Greene, Sullivan, and Ulster within the specific described boundary commonly referred to as

Owens sawmill in Arena, 1920s or 1930s. (Collection of Delaware County Historical Association)

the "blue line" (see Appendix B). ECL Section 9-0105 gives land acquisition and property management authority to NYSDEC, and Section 9-0301 states that forest preserve lands are to be maintained for the free use of the people of the state (although fees can be charged for "services rendered or facilities provided"), and prevents the diminution of the Catskill Park unless the law doing so is "enacted by the legislature at two successive regular sessions." State law reinforces and adds specificity to the constitutional protection of the forest preserve by prohibiting residential or commercial development, agriculture, timbering, mining, and dumping on forest preserve lands (Section 9-0303); limiting the placement and style of signs within the Adirondack and Catskill parks (Section 9-0305); and prohibiting transfer or lease of lands except for certain small parcels of detached forest preserve outside the Adirondack and Catskill parks (Section 9-0307).

State Environmental Conservation Law also addresses some of the rules and regulations pertaining to public use of state lands. Part 190 of Title Six of state law stipulates that camping is prohibited within 150 feet of a road, trail, stream, spring, pond, or other water body unless specifically designated by the NYSDEC as a camping site. Camping and fires are not allowed on forest preserve lands above 3,500 feet elevation, except between December 21st and March 21st, and no camping is permitted in any one location for more than four consecutive nights. Furthermore, groups of ten or more people may not camp together in one location, except by permit. The cutting of live trees in the forest preserve for firewood or any other purpose is prohibited, as is littering or burying of trash, defacing signs or other state property, removal or destruction of plants or minerals, molestation of wildlife, and public motor vehicle use (except in public campgrounds or by special permit for people with disabilities).

Constitutional and legal protections, limitations, and authorizations provide the backbone of forest preserve management; however, additional specific management and planning documents are required to establish some level of uniformity to the management of state lands throughout the park and provide day-to-day management guidance for NYSDEC personnel in specific locations. Such guidance is provided by the Catskill Park State Land Master Plan for all Catskill forest preserve lands, and by unit management plans for each individual unit of forest preserve. The Catskill Park State Land Master Plan is a blueprint and guideline for the long-term, uniform management of Catskill forest preserve lands. It was first approved and released by NYSDEC in May 1985, and incorporated many of the forest preserve classification and management recommendations suggested by the Temporary State Commission to Study the Catskills and the NYSDEC 'Catskill Task Force' working in the early 1970s. One of the primary recommendations of the commission and the task force was to classify the forest preserve lands into four separate categories for management purposes: wilderness, wild forest, intensive use, and administrative. The wilderness designation for the Catskills had actually been in consideration for quite some time, and was first proposed in 1960–61 by the New York State Joint Legislative Committee on Natural Resources. These recommended management classifications were ultimately incorporated into the 1985 Catskill Park State Land Master Plan and have been in use ever since.

The Catskill Park State Land Master Plan states that:

A fundamental determinant of land classification is the physical characteristics of the land or water, which have a direct bearing upon the capacity of the land to accept human use. … Biological considerations also play an important role in the structuring of

Inside the Eureka sawmill, late 1800s.
(Collection of Town of Neversink)

the classification system. … In addition, another significant determinant of land classification involves certain intangible considerations that have an inevitable impact on the character of the land. Some of these are social or psychological—such as the sense of remoteness and degree of wildness available to users of a particular area, which may result from the size of an area, the type or density of its forest cover, the ruggedness of the terrain or merely the views over other areas of the park obtainable from some vantage point. Without these elements an area should not be classified as wilderness, even though the physical or biological factors would dictate that the limitations of wilderness management are essential. Finally the classification system takes into account the established facilities on the land, the uses now being made by the public and the policies followed by the department. Many of these factors are self-evident: the presence of an existing campground or ski area requires the classification of intensive use.

The master plan provides a management definition for each of the four forest preserve classifications. Wilderness areas are to be preserved as they now exist and are governed by nature. They are defined as:

An area where the earth and its community of life are untrammeled by

A Catskill Park
Portfolio

The running quotation on the following pages is from the poem "The Wild" by Thomas Cole.

Upper Kaaterskill Clove, near Haines Falls (Thomas Teich)

Friends of my heart, lovers of nature's works,
Let me transport you to those wild, blue mountains
That rear their summits near the Hudson's wave.

Left: Early Spring, Notch Lake, Stony Clove (Thomas Teich); Top: Blue Mountain Scene (Frank Knight);
Above: Wittenberg Mountain from the Summit of Cornell Mountain (Thomas Teich).

Though not the loftiest that begirt the land,
They yet sublimely rise, and on their heights
Your souls may have a sweet foretaste of heaven,
And traverse wide the boundless. From this rock,
The nearest to the sky, let us look out
Upon the earth, as the first swell of day
Is bearing back the duskiness of night.

Above: Sunrise through Haines Falls Bridge (Mark McCarroll); Right: Autumn, Colgate Lake, East Jewett (Thomas Teich).

But lo, a sea of mist o'er all beneath;
An ocean, shoreless, motionless and mute.
No rolling swell is there, no sounding surf;

Left: Wild Field and Spruce Trees below Sugarloaf Mountain (Thomas Teich); Above: Evergreens, Boulder, Cliff Edge (Thomas Teich); Right: Pond in Frost Valley (Frank Knight).

Above: Sunlight in Forest (Chris Olney); Right: Birch Roots, Boulder, Stream (Thomas Teich).

Silent and solemn all;—
  the stormy main
To stillness frozen,
  whilst the crested waves
Leap'd in the whirlwind,
  and the loosen'd foam
Flew o'er the angry deep.

Far left: Water-cut Ravine, Upper Platte Clove (Thomas Teich); Left: Wild Azalea, Oak, Cliffs, Northern Platte Clove (Thomas Teich); Below: Bluestone Boulder (Chris Olney).

See! Now ascends
The lord of day, waking with heavenly fire
The dormant depths. See how his luminous breath
The rising surges kindles: lo, they heave
Like golden sands upon Sahara's gales.
Those airy forms, disparting from the mass,
Like winged ships sail o'er the marvellous plain.

Above: Stream, Autumn Trees and Sky (Thomas Teich); Right: The Five Cascades (Thomas Teich).

Clockwise from upper left: Red Trillium (Aaron Bennett); Trout Lily; Pine Cone; Fiddleheads; Pitcher Plants (Chris Olney).

Above: View from North Point (Francis X. Driscoll); Left: View from Slide Mountain (Frank Knight).

Beautiful vision! Now the veil is rent,
And the coy earth her virgin bosom bare
Slowly unfolding to the enraptured gaze
Her thousand charms.

2004 map. (NYSDEC)

The Catskill Park

Delhi

6

2

28

10

Andes

1

49

BELLEA
SKI CE

Arkville

Fleisch

30

37

Dry
Brook
Ridge
3440

49A

BEAR
SPRING

206

Mapledale

Dry Brook
Ridge
Wild Forest

Pepacton

Reservoir

30

Campbell Mt
2353

Brock Mt
2860

Mary Smith
Hill
2767

Middle Mt
2975

LITTLE
POND

Balsam
Lake Mt
3720

Balsam Lake
Mountain
Wild Forest

Doubletop
3860

Turnwood

Cherry Ridge
Wild Forest

54

Big
Wild

30

Lewbeach

SULLIVAN CO.

Mongaup Mt
3177

Hardenburgh

7
206

152

BEAVERKILL

MONGAUP
POND

17

Quick
Lake

Waneta
Lake

47

Willowemoc
Wild Forest

151

State
Fish
Hatchery

Willowemoc

Claryville

Roscoe

DELAWARE CO.

82

Debruce

81

Denman Mt
3053

19

Crystal Lake
Wild Forest

17

Grahamsville

55

42

Liberty

Wild Forest		Trails	- - - - -	**NY State** Developed Campground
Wilderness		Snowmobile		
Intensive Use		Parking	**P**	Observation (Fire) Tower
Other State Land		Roads		Information Board
		State Route (28)	County Route 42	Tourist-Visitor Center

0   5   10   Kilometers

0   5   10   Miles

Produced By: GIS Section
Division of Lands & Forests, Bureau of Public Lands

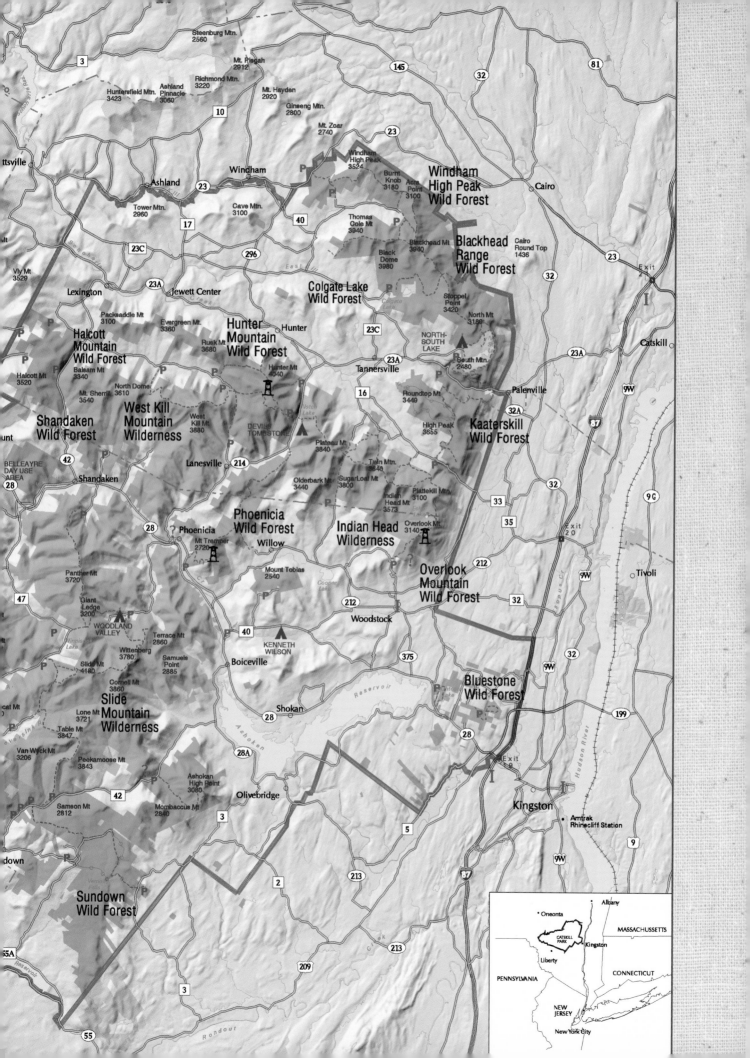

O, for an hour
Upon that sacred hill that I might sleep,
And with poetic fervour wake inspired!
Then would I tell how pleasures spring like flowers
Within the bosom of the wilderness;

Above: Schoharie Creek, Autumn, near Lexington (Thomas Teich); Right: Autumn Maple, Kaaterskill Falls (Thomas Teich).

Autumn Forest on the Trail to Twin Mountain (Thomas Teich)

And call from crumbling
    fanes my fellow-men
To kneel in nature's
    everlasting dome,
Where not the voice of
    feeble man does teach,
But His, who in the
    rolling thunder speaks,
Or in the silence of
    tenebrious night
Breathes in his power
    upon the startled ear.

Left: Spruce Forest, Tree Roots, Autumn (Thomas Teich); Above: Burnt Knob, Windham High Peak, from Acra Point (Thomas Teich); Below: Birch Grove, Autumn Light (Thomas Teich).

Then would I tell the seasons' change:
　　　　　　—how spring
　　With tears and smiles
speeds up the mountain side,
　　　　And summer sips
the moisture of her steps;—

*Right: View from Panther
Mountain (Aaron Bennett);
Below: Ashokan Reservoir in
Winter (Aaron Bennett);
Far right: Weathered Pine at
Sunset, Kaaterskill Clove
(Thomas Teich).*

Summit Forest, Snowstorm, Hunter Mountain (Thomas Teich)

*Far left: Ice Formation,
Upper Falls, Kaaterskill
Falls (Thomas Teich);
Left: Ashokan Reservoir
and Southern Catskills
(Thomas Teich); Below:
View of Slide Mountain
from Wittenberg
Mountain (Chris Olney).*

Tell how rich autumn, decked in coloured robe,
Laughing at thirsty summer, ceaseless shakes
The juicy fruits from her luxurious lap;—
And winter, rending in his angry mood,
With cold remorseless hands, the mantle bright
His dying sister left him, rudely sweeps
His snowy beard o'er all the beauteous world.

Left: Hudson Valley from Platte Clove (Francis X. Driscoll); Below: Catskill Mountain Sunset (Mark McCarroll); Right: Curved Maple, Autumn Forest Detail (Thomas Teich).

The sun was set in peace. It was the hour
When all things have a tone of sadness;—when
The soft cloud moves not on its azure bed,
Left by the purple day to fade and die,
But beautiful and lovely in its death
As is the virgin who has died of love.

Thomas Cole

Weeping Waterfall,
Upper Platte Clove
(Thomas Teich)

man—where man himself is a visitor who does not remain. A wilderness is further defined to mean an area of state land or water having a primeval character, without significant improvements or permanent human habitation. Such an area is protected and managed so as to preserve its natural conditions. Wilderness 1) generally appears to have been affected primarily by the forces of nature, with the imprint of man's work substantially unnoticeable; 2) offers opportunities for solitude or a primitive and unconfined type of recreation; 3) has at least ten thousand acres of land (and/or water) or is of sufficient size and character as to make practicable its preservation and use in an unimpaired condition; and 4) may also contain ecological, geological or other features of scientific, educational, scenic or historic value.

The master plan further states that "The primary wilderness management guidelines will be to achieve and perpetuate a plant and animal community where man's influence is not apparent." Today the Catskill forest preserve consists of approximately 119,000 acres of designated wilderness area.

According to the Catskill State Land Master Plan, "The management objective for wild forest is to accommodate present and future public recreation needs in a manner consistent with Article XIV of the state constitution." Wild forest areas are defined as:

A section of Forest Preserve where the resource can sustain a somewhat higher degree of human use than a wilderness area. It may contain, within its bounds, smaller areas of land or water that are essentially wilderness in character, where the fragility of the resource or other factors require wilderness management. A wild forest area is further defined as an area which lacks the sense of remoteness of wilderness areas and which permits a wider variety of outdoor recreation. The primary wild forest management guideline will be to protect the natural wild forest setting and to provide those types of outdoor recreation that the public can enjoy without impairing the wild forest atmosphere or changing the character of fragile areas within wild forest boundaries.

Today the Catskill forest preserve consists of approximately 157,000 acres of designated wild forest.

Intensive use areas are defined in the State Land Master Plan as:

A location where the State provides facilities for highly concentrated forms of outdoor recreation including facilities designed to accommodate significant numbers of visitors such as campgrounds, ski centers, and visitor information centers. These areas provide for congregations and/or accommodations of vis-

existing snowmobile trails give the rule less integrity. In preparing the updated master plan, the state proposed a number of other simultaneous changes and safeguards in the new master plan to offset the repeal of the 2,700 foot rule and avoid adverse impacts to forest preserve natural resources.

Most significant of these proposed changes is the creation of one new wilderness area and the expansion of another, pre-existing wilderness area by reclassifying several areas of former wild forest into wilderness. If the recommendations are adopted in the final master plan as proposed, the new wilderness area will be the Windham-Blackhead Range Wilderness Area, consisting of approximately 18,000 acres and composed of the former Blackhead Range Wild Forest, North Mountain Wild Forest, portions of the Wind- ham High Peak Wild Forest (the remaining portion of which will now be called the Elm Ridge Wild Forest), and the Blackdome Valley Wild Forest (the remaining portion of which will now be called the Colgate Lake Wild Forest). Additionally, a significant part of the Hunter Mountain Wild Forest, as well as all of the old Ox Clove Wild Forest and most of the Peck Hollow Wild Forest, will be appended to the Westkill Mountain-North Dome Wilderness Area. This will then be renamed the Hunter-Westkill Wilderness Area and consist of approximately 27,000 acres. The area around the Hunter Mountain fire tower, the "Colonel's Chair," and the trail from Spruceton Valley will remain wild forest and be renamed the Rusk Mountain Wild Forest (of approximately 3,900 acres).

Risley lumber mill in Oliverea, mid to late 1800s. (Collection of Lonnie and Peg Gale)

Another proposed safeguard for the forest preserve in the new master plan is a blanket ban on any new snowmobile trails above 3,100 feet elevation on any category of forest preserve land. This would ensure maximum protection of such places as Dry Brook Ridge and Balsam Lake Mountain. The new master plan also proposes to limit the activity of mountain biking to designated, marked trails in wild forest and intensive use areas, and prohibit that activity in wilderness areas. This potential restriction has caused more public controversy and opposition than the repeal of the 2,700 foot rule, and ongoing discussions among various stakeholder groups about the proposed mountain biking restrictions in the Catskill forest preserve has delayed the release of a final master plan. It is likely that the proposed restrictions on mountain bikes will be revised before the final master plan is adopted. Other proposed changes found in the revised master plan include stricter limitations on maximum group camping sizes in both wild forest and wilderness areas (with the new limits to be 12 people in wilderness areas and 20 people in wild forest areas); a recommendation for the official closure and abandonment of certain unused public roads through wilderness areas; updated lists of "conforming" and "non-conforming" structures in intensive use areas; and new guidance related to public education/interpretation, design standards, partnerships, and a balanced approach to recreational development. The state has been considering all public comment on the draft master plan and is expected to release the final version of the revised Catskill Park State Land Master Plan late in 2004.

The Catskill Park State Land Master Plan, both the original and as revised, calls for the preparation and implementation of unit

Family cutting wood in Johnson Hollow, circa 1900. (Collection of Larry Tompkins)

management plans (UMP's) for each of the individual units of Catskill forest preserve. UMP's provide the specific details for each area of state land, while at the same time providing some semblance of uniformity to forest preserve management and resource protection in all areas. Each of the five Catskill wilderness areas, eighteen wild forest areas, and nine intensive use areas has, or will have, their own unit management plan (the numbers of different unit types will change if the recommendations for revised classifications proposed in the draft Catskill Park State Land Master Plan are adopted in the final master plan).

Unit management plans summarize the history, natural resources, and human "improvements" for each unit of land, and are intended to guide the specific management actions for that unit for a five-year term. In wilderness and wild forest areas, a UMP will specify the locations of any new trails, designated camping sites, lean-tos, parking areas, signs and information kiosks, etc. In the intensive use areas, the recreational improvements are less primitive and designed for use by many more people, with the UMP specifying structures such as entrance booths, paved roads, graded camping spots, fire pits and grills, pavilions, docks, beaches, boat launches, dams, maintenance buildings, restrooms and sewage treatment facilities, ski lodges, chair lifts, ski slopes, etc. UMP's may also call for the removal of pre-existing human structures that are not compatible with the forest preserve, especially in wilderness areas. UMP's set forth a timeline and projected budget for the implementation of management objectives, and they also address future land acquisition priorities. A goal of each UMP is to ensure that public use of an area does not exceed the "carrying capacity" of the area, and that natural resources are not unduly compromised. Unit management plans are prepared in the regional NYSDEC offices by an interdisciplinary staff team consisting of foresters, operations people, real property specialists, and fish and wildlife biologists. Draft versions of all UMP's, as well as revisions and amendments to UMP's, are subject to public review and comment before they are finalized.

The preparation of a unit management plan requires a significant commitment of time and NYSDEC staff resources, and in all the years since the adoption of the original Adirondack and Catskill Park State Land Master Plans, the NYSDEC has still not been able to produce a UMP for every one of the Adirondack and Catskill units of forest preserve. To date, however, land managers for the Catskill forest preserve have been able to complete UMP's in a more timely fashion than their counterparts in the Adirondacks, and have released final UMP's for all but a few of the Catskill forest preserve units. Furthermore, several of the UMP's have been revised or amended since their original release (although in most cases there are not enough resources to meet the five-year update schedule recommended in the Catskill Park State Land Master Plan). New York Governor George Pataki has made a recent pledge to emphasize the completion and updating of UMP's in the Adirondacks and Catskills.

Completion of a unit management plan and incorporating public input is only the first, primary step in managing a unit of state land. Once the plan is established it must then be implemented. This is done mostly by NYSDEC staff and often under tight budget constraints. Proper management of nearly 300,000 acres of forest preserve in the Catskills requires the coordinated efforts of regional administrators and decision makers, foresters, biologists, real property specialists, surveyors, grounds and operations personnel, forest rangers, environmental conservation officers, attorneys, and seasonal employees. Trails and other recreational improvements need to be built and maintained. Fish and game laws need to be enforced. People need to be warned against and held responsible for the abuses they knowingly inflict (ex., littering, vandalism, or tree cutting) and educated about abuses they may unknowingly inflict (ex., soil compaction, erosion, or wildlife disturbance) on the natural resources of our public lands. Occasionally, lost or injured hikers or hunters need to be rescued. Forest fires need to be controlled. Rules and management guidelines will have to evolve as times change. Additional lands will be purchased. Also, the forest preserve does not exist in a vacuum; state land boundaries need to be carefully marked and re-marked to distinguish the forest preserve from neighboring private lands and help prevent abuses such as timber theft.

The stewardship demands of our state lands often outstrip the available funding, and the work of forest rangers and paid professional trail crews must be supplemented by the assistance of volunteers from hiking clubs and other civic groups. By taking on tasks such as maintaining trails, keeping lean-tos in good repair, and providing information and interpretation to visitors at popular hiking destinations such as the Catskill fire towers, volunteers become ever more valuable and appreciated. The state encourages such volunteerism by administering an Adopt-A-Natural-Resource program and providing liability insurance for volunteer trail work and other stewardship activities.

Given the special status of constitutional protection afforded to the New York State Forest Preserve and the value of this asset to the people of the state, there is much interest by nonprofit organizations and concerned citizens in ensuring that sound management decisions are made and conducted by NYSDEC personnel on forest preserve lands. Over the years, groups such as the Association for the Protection of the Adirondacks, The Adirondack Council, Adirondack Mountain Club, NY/NJ Trail Conference, Catskill 3500 Club, The Nature Conservancy, and The Catskill Center for Conservation and Development have influenced management policy and closely monitored management decisions and on-the-ground activities on forest preserve lands to ensure compliance with the constitution's "forever wild clause," the State Land Master Plan, and the individual unit management plans. These groups and others regularly provide constructive input in the unit management planning process, as well as revisions to the NYS Open Space Plan and the Adirondack and Catskill Park State Land

Master Plans. Representatives of these and other organizations also serve on an official Forest Preserve Advisory Committee, convened by NYSDEC for the purpose of collecting constructive input on a variety of issues relating to the forest preserve. The state also hears from municipalities on local issues, and from special interest groups who lobby for increased access for particular user groups such as snowmobilers, bicyclists, or people with disabilities

The Association for the Protection of the Adirondacks is the one organization whose mission focuses solely on maintaining the integrity and constitutional protection of New York's forest preserve, in both the Adirondacks and Catskills (despite their name), and their newsletter is appropriately titled *The Forest Preserve*. The association has taken the lead in sponsoring wilderness roundtables and training forums that involve a wide diversity of stakeholders including conservation professionals, land managers, people managers, outdoor recreation advocates, wilderness advocates, minority advocates, biologists, foresters and other natural resources specialists, and others from around New York and around the world. The association has been especially instrumental in advancing wilderness management training by helping to connect wilderness managers from NYSDEC with professionals and academics from the Arthur Carhart National Wilderness Training Center and various universities, along with experienced wilderness management colleagues from the National Park Service and other federal agencies.

Private Lands

When considering land management within the whole Catskill Park, one must also consider the stewardship of the private lands that comprise more than half of the land in the park. As in other places across the state, privately owned lands take the shape of tiny commercial and residential parcels in hamlets and village centers, homes scattered across the countryside and along the major roads on a few acres, private farms and forest land on several hundred acres, a few great estates with acreages in the thousands, and everything in between. The landowners themselves are equally mixed, ranging from vacationers, newcomers, and second-homeowners to people whose families have lived here for generations. Most of the heavily extractive natural resource industries that had their peak in the mid to late 1800s are long since gone; however, managed woodlots on private land remain important for their contribution of valuable firewood and timber, and there is still a small bluestone quarrying industry. The greater Catskill region also still contains much important farmland, especially in parts of Delaware, Sullivan, and Schoharie counties. Most of the private land within the more limited, mountainous area of the Catskill Park, however, is primarily residential, commercial businesses, or private forest land where most farming was abandoned long ago. Because of the close proximity to the metropolitan area of New York City and northern New Jersey, a substantial percentage—perhaps 50 percent or more in some places—of the homes and private property in the towns around the Catskill Park are now owned as second homes and weekend residences by people from those metropolitan areas.

So, when one flies over the Catskill Park one will see a heavily forested landscape, broken mostly only in the valleys where roads follow streams and connect villages and homes. Many homeowners maintain remnants of the open meadows and fields that were so common in days gone by, and these often provide the best views of surrounding mountains, create habitat diversity

Late-1800s logging crew. (Collection of Larry Tompkins)

Building the dam at Colgate Lake, circa 1920. (Collection of Larry Tompkins)

for wildlife, and add tremendously to the scenic beauty of the region. The northern hardwood forest, however, remains dominant, and its ownership is split between the state forest preserve and adjacent private woodlands. The overall mix of public and private forest land ownership is a benefit to the region for the different opportunities it provides. The forest preserve lands provide the various benefits of wilderness, and they will eventually constitute one of the largest areas of contiguous old growth forest in the eastern United States. The private forest lands in the Catskill Park, conversely, can be managed properly for other benefits that cannot be attained on forest preserve lands. Timber and other forest products such as maple syrup, mushrooms, and ginseng can

provide income for landowners and contribute to the local economy. Firewood can be collected from private woodlots to heat homes. The long-term health and economic value of a private woodlot can be improved through selective (or "selection") cutting and thinning, and wildlife habitat can be manipulated on private land to attract or benefit certain species. Meadows can be maintained and ponds can be dug on private lands, adding to the aesthetic value of a home, attracting wildlife, and giving pleasure to its landowners. The Catskill Park is richer for having both public forest preserve and private forest and farmland contributing different benefits.

Sound forest management, in particular, has become a critical component of private land stewardship in the Catskills. There is little forest land in the Catskills owned by industrial timber companies. Most of the private forest base is owned by individual private woodlot owners. The mixed hardwood forests of the Catskills generally do not lend themselves to clear-cutting, as do conifer stands in other parts of the nation, and if long-term income from timber harvesting is a goal of a landowner, then the most suitable and sustainable approach is to harvest trees selectively and carefully with future needs in mind. Many of the woodlots that were degraded in the past by poor silvicultural practices such as high-grading (taking all of the valuable or marketable trees and leaving only the poor quality trees behind) are now being healed by both time and thoughtful management (commonly referred to as "timber stand improvement" or "forest stand improvement"). More and more forest landowners are being educated on the virtues of managing their woodlots for multiple goals such as long-term forest health, income from forest products, wildlife habitat, personal recreation, aesthetics, and water quali-

ty protection. These ideals are promoted by organizations in the Catskills such as the Catskill Forest Association, the Watershed Forestry Program of the Watershed Agricultural Council, the Catskill Landowners Association, The Catskill Center for Conservation and Development, the county Cornell Cooperative Extension and Soil and Water Conservation District offices, and of course NYSDEC and NYCDEP. These groups and agencies regularly provide information and assistance to landowners. Landowners in the New York City Watershed benefit from funding programs that provide free forest management plans and other assistance relating to timber harvests and forest management.

From a distance, the forest cover of the region looks relatively continuous and uniform, obscuring the fact that the forest is divided into thousands of separate parcels of varying sizes, shapes, and owners. While our

Building the Ashokan Reservoir dam, 1907 to 1914. (Bloom Collection, courtesy Olive Free Library)

Catskill forests are not highly fragmented, from the standpoint of continuity of the forest cover, they are highly "parcelized" into many lots and varying ownerships. This parcelization and division of ownership increases as land becomes further and further subdivided, and has both positive and nega-

Bluestone has always been a signature product of the Catskill region, date unknown. (Collection of The Catskill Center)

tive consequences for private land management. Increased numbers of parcels and landowners mean that more people can enjoy living in the mountains and in close proximity to state lands, and the varying land management goals of the different owners can lead to landscape diversity, with both visual and habitat benefits. Parcels, however, can also become too small to allow for efficient and economic agriculture or forest management. Too much residential development also can erode the regional aesthetics and landscape character that draw people to the region in the first place, lead to forest fragmentation and habitat loss, and drive up the cost of municipal services.

Farmland, especially, is never fully appreciated until it is lost. In addition to the crops and animal products that feed us all, farmland provides numerous scenic and open space values that are enjoyed by the public. It has been said that the single most important product of farms, and the one that will be most missed by our society when lost, is *farm children.* Our society becomes impoverished when we lose the places that are needed to teach our children a land ethic and other values that become ever more important as they become scarcer.

Indeed, across the nation, much of today's land conservation efforts by non-profit land conservancies and, increasingly, state agencies and municipalities, are devoted to protecting the open space values of private working lands, ensuring that there will always be places to manage timber, tap maple trees, raise livestock, grow crops, and teach our children the fundamentals of caring for the land. Conservation easements, in particular, are an important tool for accomplishing many objectives that a landowner might have in common with a land conservation organization. These objectives include keeping land intact as open space; limiting and guiding future development and land uses to appropriate areas; keeping parcel sizes large enough for agricultural use or efficient forest management; encouraging sound, responsible land stewardship; maintaining scenic landscapes, including visible ridgelines and primary travel corridors; protecting wetlands and flood plains; and safeguarding wildlife habitat and other important natural features. The power of easements lies in the fact that they are usually permanent—running with the land and binding on all future owners—and they are enforced by the land conservancy, agency, or municipality holding the easement. The sale of a conservation easement can help a landowner realize some income from his or her land while keeping it in private ownership, and donating an easement can provide an income tax deduction for the donor's charitable contribution. Easements can also help lower or eliminate estate taxes, thereby being an important part of estate planning and helping to pass land on to one's heirs. Several organizations working in the central Catskills help landowners meet their conservation goals by holding conservation easements. These include NYSDEC, NYCDEP, the Watershed Agricultural Council, The Catskill Center for Conservation and Development, The Open Space Institute, The Nature Conservancy,

the Woodstock Land Conservancy, the Rondout-Esopus Land Conservancy, the Delaware Highlands Conservancy, and the Durham Valley Land Trust.

There are several ways that private lands within portions of the Catskill Park benefit from also being within the New York City Watershed, where various watershed protection partnership initiatives were funded through the 1997 New York City Watershed Memorandum of Agreement (MOA). Active farms benefit from financial assistance for "best management projects" that improve or protect water quality. Some homeowners are eligible for septic system upgrades. Communities are assisted with their sewage treatment plant, storm-water control, and municipal sand and salt storage needs. Landowners along degraded sections of streams may receive stream restoration assistance. It is clear from the New York City Watershed experience that incentive-based programs have a far more likelihood of "buy-in" and success for private land stewardship and natural resources protection than do regulatory approaches only. Additionally, a $60 million "Catskill Fund for the Future" was created in the MOA and is administered by the Catskill Watershed Corporation for the purpose of promoting environmentally friendly businesses and community development projects in the towns comprising the New York City Watershed.

A variety of resources for private land management and community planning are available in the Catskill region from the county Soil and Water Conservation Districts, Cornell Cooperative Extension offices, and planning departments, as well as from nonprofit organizations such as the Catskill Watershed Corporation, Watershed Agricultural Council, Catskill Forest Association, The Catskill Center for Conservation and Development, and the Agroforestry Resource Center.

The Future of the
Catskill Park

The early foresight in conservation that led to the Catskill Park and forest preserve has become ever more important as our national and local populations grow and our pace of land use and development quickly overruns traditional urban centers, creating problems of suburbanization and sprawling development even in rural areas. The Catskill Park and forest preserve will continue to grow in importance as part of our New York heritage. Its close proximity to huge metropolitan areas means that it will continue to be a popular recreation destination for thousands of people year-round.

The Catskill Park is not static, however; it will continue to be faced with both challenges and opportunities far into the future. One of those challenges is the development and growth of a unifying regional identity. The Catskill region is carved up by many political and administrative divisions—town and county boundaries, state agency boundaries, watershed boundaries. Coordinating the activities of different municipalities and different NYSDOT and NYSDEC regions has never been easy. The principle of "home rule" and a somewhat general aversion to regional planning make wider regional initiatives difficult to accomplish. Overcoming these hurdles will require creative solutions by government agencies, political representatives, nonprofit organizations, and the citizens of the region.

The Catskill Forest Preserve Public Access Plan is a forward-thinking blueprint and strategy for addressing needs related to the public's perception and enjoyment of the Catskill Park and forest preserve. Implementation of the public access plan's many recommendations will certainly go a long way in helping the Catskill Park realize its full potential as a regional asset. For example, one of the keys to building a better identity and awareness of the Catskill Park in the future—as outlined in the public access plan—will be better implementation of aesthetic guidelines for the travel corridors in the park. Visible park entrance signs, yellow-on-brown NYSDOT road signs, and rustic, brown box-guardrails are all important visual cues that help remind visitors and residents alike that they are in a special place. The idea of using "soft boundaries" for the Catskill Park when installing such visual cues is a good one, whereby the blue line is not strictly followed. In that way travelers aren't confused by the fact that the oddly defined park boundary crisscrosses major highways and does not have easily recognizable entry and exit points. One thus would not feel as if one entered and exited the Catskill Park several times on the drive along Route 17, Route 23, Route 28, or Route 30. This centennial year of the Catskill Park has brought recent strides in this issue with NYSDEC and NYSDOT working together to erect new Catskill Park entrance signs, and the NYSDOT working to develop an internal operating document that will help the different regions maintain consistency in their design work within the Catskill Park.

There are many other important recommendations in the Catskill Forest Preserve Public Access Plan. Completion of a Catskill Park Interpretive Center will also go a long way to address the need for a better regional identity and fill an important need for better public outreach and education. The same is true for developing new kiosks, gateway information centers, recreational brochures, maps, and universal icon markers along public roads to direct visitors to trailheads, campgrounds, public fishing areas, and other points of interest. The plan also advocates for expanded access for people with disabilities; expanded public fishing access; trail linkages to inns, villages, and NYC Watershed lands; enhanced year-round recreation at the Belleayre Ski Area; and establishment of a NYSDEC Catskills coordinator position to improve communication and cooperation between the agency's two separate offices responsible for the Catskill forest preserve (Region 3 and Region 4). The potential for linkages between state lands and lands acquired by NYCDEP within the NYC Watershed is particularly great with the city

continuing to purchase thousands of acres, much of which border forest preserve lands and offer new recreational opportunities and improved public access.

Few good solutions to regional challenges and problems come from the top down; in fact, most are generated from citizen input and participation. In the Catskill Park there is no overriding regional land use planning agency that regulates land use analogous to the Adirondack Park Agency. Unlike in the Adirondacks, the Catskill Park sign law remains the only state-imposed land use regulation on private lands within the Catskill Park. There is no difference between private land inside the Catskill Park and private land outside the Catskill Park, except for the limitation on signs and outdoor advertising. Therefore, no matter how many effective organizations there are that educate landowners and communities about natural resource protection and sustainable development, the real successes in private land stewardship ultimately come from the decisions made by each individual landowner, business owner, or community. Landowners can choose to keep their property intact and managed in environmentally friendly ways that meet long-term goals. They can hire a forester to guide the actions of the logger. They can choose to place their dream house in the edge of the woods rather than in the middle of the big meadow, and they can use colors and styles that are consistent with the rural character of their surroundings.

Business owners can choose to locate their business in the established hamlets and villages rather than in the scenic open spaces along primary travel corridors. They can choose not to advertise on billboards that are inconsistent with the Catskill park sign law (but are "grandfathered in"). The beauty of nature speaks for itself; it is our human endeavors that require a measure of forethought, planning, and sensitivity if they are to compliment our natural surroundings and be attractive to ourselves and others.

Above all, communities can embrace the wilderness provided by the forest preserve and the uniqueness of their place in the park as part of their heritage and appeal. They can capitalize on this great asset by adopting a regional identity and vision, promoting the opportunities afforded by the Catskill forest preserve, and being proud of their place in or

Plowing through the deep snow of Stony Clove, 1920. (Collection of Larry Tompkins)

around the Catskill Park. Municipalities in and around the park should take more interest in supporting the types of measures outlined in the Catskill Forest Preserve Public Access Plan. They can partner with NYS-DEC to build and maintain trailhead parking areas, kiosks, and other improvements, and even help establish trails that link state land to village centers, inns, and other points of interest. Municipalities can also take measures, such as conforming to the yellow-on-brown sign colors on local town roads in the Catskill Park to reinforce state efforts to create the visual appeal critical for making good first impressions on the visitors that are crucial to the tourism component of the regional economy. The Town of Hunter, for example, has been a leader when it comes to forming partnerships with the state to enhance public access to the forest preserve. This partnership has created new parking areas and helped make the North-South Lake Campground accessible year-round. It is this type of mutually beneficial relationship between the state, local municipalities, and even businesses that should be explored and encouraged throughout the Catskill Park.

At a Catskill forest preserve forum in 1997, ecologist and environmental economics consultant Dr. Paul Kerlinger told his audience that nature-based tourism, agri-tourism, and cultural tourism, as well as the attraction of small businesses such as antique stores, craft shops, and bed and breakfasts are an under-utilized economic resource in the Catskills. He suggested that the challenge is to capitalize on regional assets such as the NYC Watershed and the Catskill forest preserve without degrading the resource. These same sentiments have been echoed in various regional planning documents for the Catskills. While some would argue that we should keep our secret to ourselves and not promote the virtues of the Catskill region, it is largely sound advice to look to an economic future of small, sustainable businesses that capitalize on the beauty of an area to which people will always be attracted. We have the power to create unique communities with beauty, value, and appeal; or alternatively we can allow our neighborhoods to succumb to the unplanned pressures that erode local identity, compromise environmental integrity, and diminish the allure and respectability of a place for residents and visitors alike. The challenge has been, and will continue to be, for the people of the Catskills to maintain their properties and develop their communities and businesses in ways that complement, rather than conflict with, the natural beauty and environmental quality of the surrounding wilderness. If we succeed, the fruits of our labors will be rewarded by an improved quality of life here in the mountains.

The people of the park must also be participants in achieving a positive future not just for their own private lands in the Catskill Park, but also for the forest preserve. People who appreciate and use the forest preserve need to make their voices heard and be advocates for better state funding for land protection, outdoor recreation opportunities, and other open space resources, as well as adequate

personnel to meet public land management and stewardship needs. Volunteerism, however, will continue to be critical for maintaining and enhancing the quality of our hiking trails and other recreational resources in the forest preserve and on other state lands. Forest rangers not only need physical stewardship assistance, but also assistance in informing visitors about the proper use of our public lands, as well as the prevention of overuse and habitat degradation. Learning the principles of "Leave No Trace" and passing them on to others can be the best way to give something back to the natural areas that we value so much. It is also important that an informed and concerned public take the initiative to review and offer constructive comment on management proposals in any number of unit management plans and other guiding documents. There will always be times when we are called on to make tough judgments about what management activities and what recreational uses are appropriate in the forest preserve in general, or more specifically in wilderness areas vs. wild forest areas vs. intensive use areas. Answering the tough questions about how to balance public recreation demands, public safety, and unspoiled wilderness values and wilderness experiences will never be easy and will always require informed dialogue.

Similarly, the people of the state, who collectively own the forest preserve, must always be ready to act in its best interest, to defend the integrity of the forest preserve, and to guard the protections afforded it by our state constitution and state laws. Those who see the forest preserve as a wasted or unutilized, unmanaged resource that should be harvested of its timber and other extractable resources do not appreciate the values of wilderness, whether economic, philosophical, or spiritual. They believe in a false economy. Managed landscapes certainly serve very important purposes and must be noted for their own values, but not at the expense of our forever wild lands. Ed Zahniser, of the National Park Service and son of wilderness lobbyist Howard Zahniser, stated at a 1997 Wilderness Roundtable sponsored by the Association for the Protection of the Adirondacks, "Wilderness preservation and wilderness management are not about natural resources; wilderness preservation and wilderness management are about the social contract." Our society should not allow the surrender of the few places of wilderness that we have managed to preserve. There needs to be increased education of the public as to the merits and inherent values of wilderness. This sentiment was summed up succinctly by lawyer and environmentalist Alfred Forsyth when he wrote about New York's forest preserve in *The Forest and The Law:* "Perhaps the clearest lesson to be learned from this review of legislative history is that eternal vigilance is the price of preservation."

The Association for the Protection of the Adirondacks has been hard at work creating the "Center for the Forest Preserve," which will serve coming generations as an Adirondack and Catskill forest preserve research library, document and photograph archive, and meeting and discussion place for forest preserve issues. The Center for the Forest Preserve is located in the former home of lifelong Adirondack conservation leader and

forest preserve defender Paul Schaefer in Niskayuna, New York. The research library boasts an incredible collection of information and is made accessible to the public by trained volunteers. This fantastic resource will only grow and mature as a complete and useful library, and it will surely help inspire and educate many future New York conservation leaders.

Other far-reaching questions remain regarding the Catskill Park. With such an oddly defined boundary, is there a chance that the blue line will ever be redefined to encompass a more logical land area? Perhaps someday the park boundary will be expanded again, possibly following more natural landscape features such as watershed boundaries and encompassing more of what can be considered the Catskill region proper. There are, of course, pros and cons to such a change. A new boundary might simply "make more sense" because it follows more intuitive boundaries and encompasses more of the central mountain area of the region. It would provide the opportunity to protect more land as wilderness; however, there may be some areas of public land that are better left as reforestation areas or wildlife management areas because of the management flexibility afforded by those designations. Some businesses might resist such a change because of the sign law that would be imposed on them; however, it is arguable that a region without billboards is much more attractive to visitors and potential customers than one with "billboard blight." A revision to the blue line would require a constitutional amendment, and such a proposal would engender much debate about the merits and drawbacks of doing so.

There may be other instances where a constitutional amendment affecting the Catskill Park and/or forest preserve might be proposed. The topic of privatization of the Belleayre Ski Area occasionally comes up in local politics. In the mid-1990s the Hunter Mountain Ski Area sought a constitutional amendment that would have allowed that ski area to expand its operations onto adjacent forest preserve land in return for funding the acquisition of additional forest preserve land elsewhere. It was a very controversial proposal that was not approved. Similar propositions may be put forth in the future, but not all constitutional amendments need to be far-reaching or controversial. Some amendments may be necessary to provide *better* management for a particular public resource. For

example, in some instances when the state acquires land, they also acquire buildings or other structures that are considered "non-conforming" in the forest preserve and may be slated for demolition despite their historic or other value. This is true in the case of the historic Coykendall Mansion at Alder Lake, where demolition has been temporarily stayed while a group of concerned individuals tries to create a restoration plan and raise funds. Outside of Pine Hill, the state received a gift of land from the Reisser family, along with a beautiful farmhouse, barn, and other buildings. The state's ability to care for and properly utilize these buildings, and even to maintain the property as anything but forest, is quite limited under its classification as forest preserve. The potential of assets such as these might be better realized under the care of a nonprofit organization; however, such a change in ownership in the forest preserve would require a constitutional amendment.

Train coming into Haines Falls, early 1900s. (Collection of Larry Tompkins)

Another interesting question to ponder is the future condition of the recovering wilderness lands of the forest preserve. Today we are used to seeing a slowly maturing forest that still shows many signs of the past human disturbances that affected them—stumps, log roads, even-age compositions, transitional species, stone walls, and old building foundations. But in a couple of hundred years we will have old growth again and a much different forest than yesterday or today. Will this old growth forest of the Catskills be the same as it was in pre-colonial times? It would be tempting to think that it might be, but an accounting of several influencing factors would indicate otherwise. Even by keeping large tracts of forest land free from management and direct human disturbance, it will never, short of a returning ice age, achieve its pre-colonial condition because of the pressures and influences of things such as past land use, acid precipitation, climate change, invasive species, and pathogens. There is already much evidence that the composition of the Catskill forests is changing, as acid rain leaches nutrients from the soil, as pests and pathogens weaken or kill off certain tree species, and as excessive browsing from an overpopulation of deer hinders forest regeneration. The American chestnut, which was so common in the past, was lost from our forests nearly a hundred years ago. Today the eastern hemlock is threatened by the hemlock woolly adelgid, and the American beech suffers from beech bark disease. Other exotic forest invaders loom on the horizon. Many factors will determine the condition of the future Catskill forests, but it is safe to say that the forests of the future are unlikely to resemble those that the Native Americans encountered on their hunting expeditions into the Catskill Mountains.

The Catskill Park is unquestionably a unique area of New York and of the United Sates. It is an area that has a long and colorful history and is increasingly entering the focus of public attention. The mountains and valleys of the Catskills have many geological, ecological, historical, cultural, and social lessons to teach those who have the patience to learn. Few would dispute that the natural areas of the Catskills are both rugged and raw, yet invigorating, inspirational, and remedial. The magnificent and expansive grandeur of other, taller, mountainous areas of the country may shake you by the shirt collar and make your eyes light up, but the more subtle, "deep beauty" of the Catskills is equally attractive in a different way, and it will creep into your bones and stay there forever.

Appendix A

Charles Carpenter
1886 Report to the
State Forest Commission
on the Catskill Preserve

Reprinted from Second Annual Report
of the Forest Commission

The Catskill Preserve

During the past winter the Commission detailed Inspector Charles F. Carpenter to make a thorough examination of the Catskill Preserve. His report, presented herewith, is based on a careful personal inspection of that region :

REPORT OF INSPECTOR CARPENTER ON THAT PORTION OF THE FOREST PRESERVE INCLUDED WITHIN THE CATSKILL DISTRICT.

The Catskill region includes portions of Greene, Ulster, Sullivan and Delaware counties. In location it occupies a large part of the south-eastern corner of the State. The valley of the Hudson river forms its eastern border. The rich agricultural lands of Orange county, and the wild mountain regions of Pike and Wayne counties of Pennsylvania coming down the Delaware river, form its southern boundary. Broome, Chenango, Otsego, Schoharie and Albany counties, including a rich agricultural section, principally devoted to hop raising and dairy products, bound the Catskills on the west and north. From the Hudson river the mountains are distant about nine miles, and occupy a position very nearly parallel with its course.

The central point of this region lies somewhere in the town of Hardenburgh, in Ulster county, in about latitude 42° north and longitude 2° 30' east from Washington, and about 100 miles distant from Albany and sixty miles from New York City. A circle about fifty miles in diameter struck from this point will include nearly the whole of this Catskill mountain region, with, however, the addition of an arm including the towns of Hunter, Jewett, Windham and Cairo, in Greene County, projecting north-easterly, and another arm including the southern-most towns of Sullivan county, forming a projection due south from the center of the circle, comprising altogether an area of about 2,500 square miles.

The contour of this mountain district is extremely diversified, possessing every feature known to hill and valley; on the eastern face of the Catskills the slope is generally towards the north and east, and the streams taking these directions find their way to the Hudson river. There is a large interior watershed, hemmed by a circle of high peaks and mountain ranges. Starting from a point in the Plattekill Clove, the dividing ridge on the south is marked by Sugar Loaf mountain, Plateau mountain, Hunter mountain, Big Westkill mountain, North Dome, Mount Sheril, Vly mountain, Bloomberg mountain, Irish mountain, Bald mountain, Mount Utsayantha, Mine mountain, Woodchuck mountain, till the peaks fall away and form the Schoharie hills. Returning to the same point in the Plattekill Clove, the dividing ridge includes High Peak, Round top, Haines's Falls divide and Stoppel Point. From this last the mountain ranges, with well-defined crests, have been made the dividing line between the towns of Cairo and Durham on the north, and Jewett and Windham on the south in Greene county, terminating at Mount Pisgah at the south-east corner of Schoharie county. From this point the range continues to waste away, finding its last eminence in Leonard hill, near the center of Schoharie county. From the slopes of this interior basin the waters of the Schoharie creek take rise and gather strength and volume for their long circuit, and finally, after mingling with the waters of the Mohawk, and in turn with the Hudson, find themselves, when opposite Saugerties, only ten miles from their starting point. The waters

coming from the southern slope of the mountains, on reaching the lower slopes, take an easterly course and flow into the Hudson river; those from the general western slope form the several branches which together make up the headwaters of the Delaware river. The Hudson river slope is by far the greatest, occupying as it does a large portion of the three counties of Greene, Ulster and Sullivan. Next in importance is the Delaware slope, and wedged in between the two is the basin of the Schoharie creek. These two main slopes, and the interior basin, are divided into innumerable smaller systems, but the streams from them all find each their own channel at last, and though they twist and turn in their tortuous course, traversing many a mile, still the general course is towards the outlet of the water-

Browns Station, Town of Olive, circa 1910. (Bloom Collection, courtesy Olive Free Library)

HIGH PEAKS OF THE CATSKILLS.

Name of Mountain.	Town.	Elevation, in feet.
Greene County		
Hunter	Hunter	4,052
Black Dome	Windham and Jewett	4,004
Thomas Cole	do	3,975
Black Head	Cairo and Windham	3,965
Big West Kill	Lexington	3,900
Vly	Halcott and Lexington	3,888
Plateau	Hunter	3,855
Sugar Loaf or Mink	do	3,807
Kaaterskill High Peak	do	3,800
Twin	do	3,650
Indian Head	do	3,581
Windham High Peak	Windham and Durham	3,534
Round Top	Hunter	3,500
North	do	3,450
Huntersfield	Prattsville	3,300
Mount Richmond	Ashland	3,202
Colonel's Chair	Hunter	3,200
Plattekill	do	3,200
East Kill	do	3,190
Jewett	Jewett	3,025
Tower	do	2,931
Mount Pisgah	Windham	2,905
Mount Hayden	do	2,900
South	Hunter	2,500
Clum Hill	do	2,372
Pine Orchard	Catskill	2,227
Ulster County		
Slide	Shandaken	4,220
Mount Cornell	do	3,920
Graham	Hardenburgh	3,886
Peakamoose	Denning	3,875
Table	do	3,875
Wittenberg	Shandaken	3,824
Big Indian	Hardenburgh	3,800
Panther	Shandaken	3,800
Eagle	Hardenburgh	3,566
Overlook	Woodstock	3,300
High Point	Olive	3,100

Mount Garfield	Shandaken	2,650
Tysten-Eyck	Woodstock	2,600
Mount Sheridan	Shandaken	2,490
Summit	do	2,482
Mount Tobias	Woodstock	2,000
	Delaware County	
Bloomberg	Roxbury	3,456
Mount Pisgah	Delhi	3,425
Mount Utsayantha	Stamford	3,365
Bramley	Delhi	2,850
Mount McGregor	do	2,550

shed of which they form a component part, and sooner or later their waters mingle, forming one of the numerous kills in which this region abounds.

There are very few well-defined mountain ranges; the impression to the casual observer being that of a great number of peaks huddled together. Still, by a little closer examination, they can be made to conform somewhat to systematic lines. Viewed in the broadest sense, they can be considered as the foot-hills of the higher Alleghanies, and as such, a part of the great Appalachian system which forms the Atlantic slope of the continent and extends nearly parallel with the coast line from Nova Scotia to the Gulf of Mexico; of which system the Adirondack mountains do not form a part, they being of the Laurentian system.

The Catskill region is made up of rough mountain and deep valley, the very inaccessibility of which, together with the unkindly nature of the soil, has been its only salvation. Occupying but a patch on the broad domain of the whole State, insignificant in proportions when compared with the Adirondack region, thinly clothed with a forest of hard wood timber only, but maintaining an enviable position with reference to, and filled with resources commanding an active market at the shipping port of the world, this little patch is a mine of wealth and a source of vast income, both to the State and to individuals. It is, therefore, worthy of a thought how best not to waste these resources. Walton Van Loan, of Catskill, in his published *Catskill Mountain Guide*, gives the high peaks of the Catskills, which, when arranged according to the counties in which they are located, will convey a fair idea of their comparative elevations (see table above). The base of comparison is tide water to the Hudson river at the foot of the mountains.

These mountain ridges divide this region into innumerable small water-sheds, the gatherings from which contribute to comparatively few large streams. The Schoharie creek water-shed, principally in Greene county, is, in reality, made up of four or five smaller ones, being divided by spurs from the main ridges. There is a divide between the headwaters of the Schoharie creek and the West kill, the two streams coming together at Lexington; another divide starts at Stoppel Point and ends at Jewett Centre where the waters of the East kill join the Schoharie creek; another divide starts at Black Head mountain and takes nearly a due east course ending near Prattsville, where the waters of the Batavia kill join the Schoharie creek; another divide starts from the main range at the south-east corner of Schoharie county and taking a course about parallel with the last divide continues on into Delaware county; the Schoharie creek breaks through this ridge near Dewasego Falls in Schoharie county, and below this Manor kill enters the Schoharie near Gilboa in Schoharie county. Innumerable smaller streams come in from both sides of the main stream.

The eastern slope draining into the Hudson river direct four principal water-sheds. The ridge between the first water-shed, drained by the Catskill creek, which enters the Hudson river at Catskill, starts a little west of that village and follows nearly a straight line to the south-east corner of the town of Jewett at Stoppel Point mountain, thence it follows the main range to where that runs out in Schoharie county. The Kaaters kill drains the country immediately south of the Catskill water-shed and has for its southern boundary the ridge back of Saugerties, which pursues a north-east course for a distance of about five miles, then turns north-westerly to strike High Peak, Round Top and the border of the Kaaterskill Clove at Haines's Falls. South of this water-shed is the great water-shed of the Esopus creek, the

Directing traffic for the Catskill Mountain Railroad in Phoenicia. (Mark McCarroll)

north boundary of which starts in the Plattekill Clove, on either side of which within a few rods of each other are the sources of the Platte kill, a branch of the Esopus creek, and the fountain head of the Schoharie creek, the waters of which take opposite directions, each in time arriving at the same point in the Hudson river. From the summit in the Plattekill Clove the divide leads over Sugar Loaf mountain, to the summit between Roaring kill going to the Schoharie creek, and the Beaver kill going to the Esopus, thence by many twists and turns it finds its way to the Hudson near Kingston. The Beaver kill coming from the Plattekill Clove in Greene County joins the Esopus at Glenerie; the Saw kill rising in Cooper lake in the town of Woodstock, Ulster county, joins the Esopus above Kingston. Another Beaver kill rising near Sugar Loaf mountain in the town of Hunter, Greene county, within a few rods of the source of one of the headwaters of the Schoharie creek, joins the Esopus at Phoenicia. The Stony Clove creek, in the town of Shandaken, Ulster county, rising within a few miles of the village of Hunter, in Greene county, furnishing water power for an important industry, also joins the Esopus creek at Phoenicia. The Smith Bush kill rises in several diminutive ponds near the summit between the Schoharie creek water-shed and the Esopus creek water-shed, and but a few rods from where the waters of a branch of the West kill rise, flows through Bushnellville near the southerly line of the town of Lexington, Greene county, and enters the Esopus creek at Shandaken in Ulster county. Each of the above enumerated

streams has a water-shed of its own, of a greater or less magnitude and extent, the larger of them being those drained by the first mentioned Beaver kill and the Saw kill. The Rondout creek drains the water-shed on both sides of the Shawangunk range of mountains; the Rondout proper lies on the north-westerly side of the range, and the Shawangunk kill, heading within a few miles of Port Jervis, in the south-westerly corner of Orange county, lies on the south-easterly side of the range. A ridge of low hills starts near the junction of the Shawangunk kill with the Wall kill forming with the Highlands of the Hudson a narrow and abrupt water-shed drained by the Wall kill. The junction of the Shawangunk kill and the Wall kill is but a few miles north of the south line of Ulster county.

Sullivan county, with the exception of one-half of the town of Neversink, as a part of the Rondout creek water-shed, drains into the Delaware river. From the south-west corner of the county the Delaware river, which forms its southern boundary, flows in a south-easterly direction to Lackawaxen, and from this point to the south-east corner of the county the course of the river is nearly due east, continuing this direction to Port Jervis where it takes a sharp turn to the south-west, following the trend of the Shawangunk range of mountains. At this point the Neversink river joins the Delaware, flowing across the entire width of Sullivan county in a south-easterly direction. The divide between this water-shed and the water-shed of the Shawangunk kill and the Rondout creek follows the crest of the

Shawangunk mountains to Wurtsborough, and, thence along the height of land bordering the Neversink river till the headwaters are reached near the north boundary line of the town of Denning, in Ulster county. The divide between this water-shed and that of the Mongaup river follows a line nearly parallel with that between the Neversink river and Rondout creek, but reaches its highest point considerably south of the headwaters of the Neversink, this point being near the north-east corner of the town of Liberty, in Sullivan county.

From this water-shed to that of the two branches of the Callicoon creek the intervening distance is divided into several small water-sheds, all south of the south line of the Hardenburgh Patent, with the single exception of that of Ten mile creek, which extends north to about opposite the center of the east line of the town of Delaware, Sullivan county. These last are all directly tributary to the Delaware river. The water-shed of the two branches of the Callicoon creek includes a section embracing the towns of Delaware, Callicoon and the west one-third of the town of Liberty, both branches of the creek rising within a few miles of each other near the south line of the town of Rockland, Sullivan county. A mountain ridge starts at the junction of the Beaver kill with the east branch of the Delaware river and marks the southern boundary of a water-shed; another ridge starts from near the same place, and bearing to the north-east, passes into the south-western portion of the town of Hardenburgh; another ridge starts from the summit near Parksville, in the town of Liberty, Sullivan

county, and joins the second ridge in the town of Hardenburgh, near Tunis lake. The territory embraced within these limits is the watershed of the Beaver kill and its main branch, the Willewemoc. The east branch of the Delaware river has for a watershed the territory included between the north bounds of the Beaver kill water-shed, the east bounds of the Esopus creek and Schoharie creek water-sheds, and the crown of the ridge between the east branch of the Delaware river proper. The water supply in the streams and rivers is subject to the same fluctuations observed in other sections which have been partially denuded of their original timber growth and have been more or less wasted by the action of fire. Those who depend on the water in the streams to drive the machinery of their mills and factories begin to appreciate the fact that the available summer supply is steadily on the decrease. In conversation with manufacturers in various parts of this region and with people who have been long resident on the banks of the streams or in their immediate vicinity, I have heard convincing testimony as to this failure through the dry season. At a large chair factory at Chichesterville, on the Stony Clove creek, one of the officers of the company informed me that twenty-five years ago, when they first located in the place, their factory could be run entirely by water-power; now, and for several years past, they have been obliged to supplement it by the use of steam, the water having dwindled away to such an extent as to furnish through the summer months only one-half the power it formerly did. He likewise complained of being troubled with

View toward Arkville from Murray Hill, circa 1900. (Collection of Delaware County Historical Association)

floods in the spring and fall and, naturally enough, concluded his whole trouble came from cutting off the timber on the watershed of the stream, particularly at its source, and also from allowing disastrous fires to burn up the muck-soil and leaf-mold, so that nothing remained on the surface to hold back the water of rain storms, which, rushing off from a denuded and steep water-shed, caused the sudden and damaging floods in the stream. Another manufacturer, in the town of Wawarsing, Ulster county, whose factory is located on the Vernooy creek, a branch of the Rondout creek, who uses water-power from eight to nine months in the year, has used steam-power in connection with this since 1863, when the summer supply began to fail. Previous to that he used water-power

the year round. He attributes the change in the supply to cutting off the timber on some swampy pieces of land, which were filled with standing water while the timber grew there, but which dried out after it was cut down and has been dry through the summer months ever since. Examples could be multiplied all through and around this region, but inasmuch as all seem to be agreed as to the cause of the decrease of the water-supply in the dry seasons and invariably attribute it to cutting off the timber-growth, there is little need of repeating or recording them.

The Catskill region abounds in streams of large volume and rapid descent, furnishing power to a large number of manufacturing concerns, which draw their raw material, in most part, from the forests which clothe

the mountains. A continuation of these industries depends, to a large extent, on the continuance of the water supply, and that in turn depends upon a judicious management of the forests, of keeping out fires and allowing such sections as have once been cut to grow up with a new forest covering. At Chichesterville a stream comes out of a clove to the west of the main stream. The water-shed of this stream was cut clean of its timber several years ago, since which time it has grown up pretty well with small stuff, and the summer flow of this stream is greater than that of the main stream, which is a convincing fact in regard to the action of vegetation on the retention and delivery of the rain-fall.

The Hudson river receives the waters of four large and important streams, which find their rise in the Catskill mountains. The Schoharie creek, made up of the combined flow of the East kill, West kill, Batavia kill and Manor kill, flows down a steep and rugged valley, takes almost a due north course, and finally empties into the Mohawk river at Fort Hunter, in Montgomery county. This stream in the mountain regions furnishes water power for numerous manufactures, and in early times, before the hemlock timber was all cut off, many tanners prosecuted a thriving and lucrative business by aid of its water power. The valley is occupied for the greater part of its length as a farming section and through the towns of

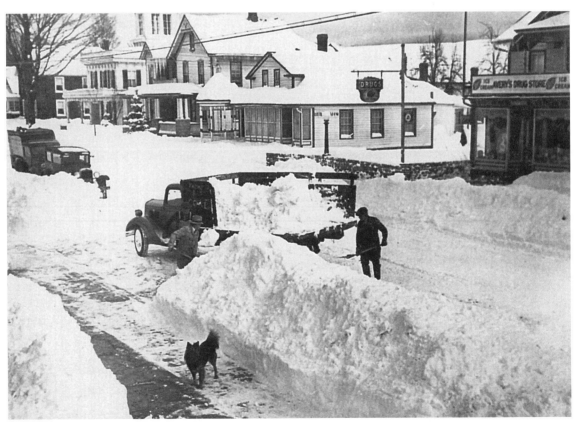

Snowy winter in Windham, late 1930s. (Collection of Larry Tompkins)

Hunter and Lexington, in Greene county, a large summer population finds accommodation in the many large hotels and boarding-houses scattered along its banks. Indeed so much attention is paid to the business of entertaining summer boarders that the farms show many signs of neglect. The land along the stream is for the most part poor and stony and the sides of the valley steep and very abrupt in places. The remaining three of the four streams going to the Hudson river reach it direct. Of these the Catskill is the furthest north; the stream proper rises in Schoharie county and flows in a south-easterly direction, being re-enforced first by the Potuck creek, coming from Albany county, and second by the Kaaterskill, rising in the town of Hunter, Greene county. It reaches the Hudson river at the Catskill village, through which it flows. Comparatively little manufacturing is done on this creek or its branches.

Next in order is the Esopus creek, which for length, strength and utility bears off the palm; manufacturing establishments of all description line its banks and prosperous, thriving villages occur at frequent intervals. The branches of this stream are rather unimportant in size, and come in mostly from the north. The stream rises in the Big Indian hollow, in the town of Shandaken, Ulster county, flows first northerly till the main valley is reached, then turns sharply toward the east, pursuing this course to Shandaken, where it gradually assumes a south-easterly course, following this direction to near the village of Stone Ridge, in the town of Marbletown, where it takes a sharp bend to the north-east

and continues thus to the city of Kingston; here its course is again changed more to the north to near the village of Saugerties, where, turning due east, it finds its way to the Hudson. The main tributaries of this stream are the Saw kill, which joins it about three miles north of Kingston, and the Platte kill, which joins it at Glenerie, forming a part of the division line between the towns of Kingston and Saugerties. Following the Esopus, in order, comes the Rondout creek, taking its rise in the high mountains near the north-east corner of the town of Denning, Ulster county. Its course is first south-westerly, traversing a portion of the north-east corner of Sullivan county, then, turning a sharp corner, it passes out of Sullivan county, in a south-easterly course until its junction is made with the Sandburgh creek; here another sharp turn to the north-east is made, which course it pursues till it empties into the Hudson river at Rondout. This stream is re-enforced by the waters of the Shawangunk Kill and the Wall kill which drain the section lying south-east of the Shawangunk range of mountains.

Down the valley of the Rondout creek the Delaware and Hudson canal has been built, affording slack water navigation from the Hudson to the Delaware, and transportation for the cement manufactured through that and the adjoining valleys, and the coal used in burning it. This is the last of the large streams coming from the Catskill, whose waters go the Hudson river; the water-shed of the Shawangunk kill being the Shawangunk range of mountains, which meeting the high ridge bordering the

Neversink forms an impassable barrier, and caused the Delaware river at Port Jervis to make an abrupt turn toward the south. If this range had not existed, the Delaware river would have been a tributary of the Hudson, finding its outlet through the valley of the Rondout creek. The Shawangunk grit proved too much for the erosive effect of water, even when thrown against it in as great a volume as that of the Delaware. The remainder of the Catskill region is drained by the Delaware river, this embraces the western and south-western mountain regions, and includes the counties of Sullivan and Delaware.

Starting from the southern end of the north and south dividing ridge, the first stream of importance is the Mongaup river, which takes its rise near the village of Parksville in the town of Liberty, Sullivan county, flows in a southerly direction across the county, and enters the Delaware at Port Jervis. This is a stream of magnitude and importance, draining a long, narrow section of territory; mostly a wild and sparsely settled country, hilly and rolling it its nature.

In the town of Fremont two unimportant streams come to the river, one at Hankins and the other at Basket near the south-west corner of the town; both rise in the northern part of the town and flow in a south-westerly direction. They are known, respectively, as Hankins creek and Basket Creek. Fremont is the south-western town of the county. Beyond this the east branch of the Delaware river joins the main stream. This branch rises near the north line of the town of Roxbury, Delaware county, follows a nearly due south course, being supplied from the east by the

Batavia kill which drains the eastern side of the town of Roxbury; the Bush kill rising near the north bounds of the town of Halcott, Ulster county; Dry brook, rising near the south-east corner of the town of Hardenburgh, Ulster county, and joining the Bush kill at the village of Arkville, in the town of Middletown, Delaware County; and lastly, the Beaver kill, with its branch, the Willewemoc, which rises in the south-western portion of the town of Denning, Ulster county, crosses the north-west corner of the town of Neversink, Sullivan county, and thence flowing in a westerly course across the town of Rockland, Sullivan county, it joins the Beaver kill near the village of Westfield Flats in the south-western part of the town. The Beaver kill proper rises near the middle of the southerly boundary of the town of Hardenburgh, Ulster county, flows in a westerly direction and passes out of the town at the north-west corner, then runs in a south-westerly direction along the boundary line of the town of Rockland, in Sullivan county, to its junction with the Willewemoc. At this point it makes a sharp turn toward the west in the general course of the Willowemoc, to its junction with the east branch of the Delaware river. The Beaver kill, with its branch the Willewemoc, forms an important water power. Its sources are among the wildest and densest forests of this region, and not far from the headwaters of the Esopus creek and the Neversink river. Near these sources is a group of mountain peaks among which are Big Indian and Double Top. From this group the streams flow to the four cardinal points of the compass. The rivulets that form Dry brook flow away from them to the north and reach the Delaware. Pigeon brook flows south to the Neversink and on to the Hudson. Elk Bush kill flows east to Big Indian Hollow, joins the Esopus and thence to the Hudson. The springs supplying Tunis lake rise in this group and follow down its western slope to issue at its foot, becoming in time the Beaver kill whose waters go to the Delaware river. Thus the circuit of the water-shed is completed. The Hudson receives by far the greater portion of the water, and would have received all but for the interposition of the flinty range of the Shawangunk mountains, which threw its barrier across the path of the Delaware and forced it to seek an outlet through another channel, and to traverse trice the distance it would have had in a straight course to the Hudson.

Ulster and Greene counties cannot lay claim to any great number of lakes or ponds, the conformation of the land favoring more the formation of streams. Such as there are have been eagerly sought out and purchased by private parties, who control and use them. They are scarcely deserving of the name of lake, which term, however, has a different signification in different localities, and of itself is no criterion of the size or magnitude of the body of water. Back of the Catskill Mountain House, in Greene county, are two lakes, known, respectively, as South lake and North lake (on the maps as the Catskill lakes), the first covering thirty-three acres and the second twenty-six acres, being at an elevation of over 2,200 feet above tide-water. They are part of the Mountain House property and a fine feature of the surroundings of that resort. In the town of Athens, Greene

Raccoon hunters in Big Hollow, 1918. (Collection of Larry Tompkins)

Village of Grahamsville, circa 1900. (Collection of Town of Neversink)

county, are Hollister lake, Green's lake, Black lake and Canoe lake, and in the town of Coxsackie is Bronk lake. This is rather a poor showing for an entire county, but the conformation of the land does not allow the accumulation of bodies of water. Ulster county makes a little better showing. Eight towns have lakes or ponds in them. The town of Hardenburgh has four lakes in it, Beecher pond, Balsam lake, Furlow lake and Tunis lake. These are all owned by private parties and held by them for their own enjoyment. Denning has two ponds, known as East pond and Round pond. Woodstock has Copperas lake, near the Overlook House, and Shues lake. Rosendale has the Binnewaters, of which there are five, in two groups. The first group embraces the first, second and third Binnewaters, and the second group the fourth and fifth Binnewaters. The water from

these lakes goes to the Rondout creek. Hurley has one, Temple pond. Marbletown has one, without a name. Rochester has Lake Mahonk, a noted summer resort. Wawarsing has three, Cape pond, Long pond and Little Mud pond. Long pond is a good-sized body of water, covering fifty or more acres and is deep, with precipitous sides.

Sullivan county is full of lakes, the lay of the land being such as to permit the formation of hollows, in which bodies of water have accumulated. Consequently there are found from one to fifteen lakes in every town of the county, but none of them very large. They are distributed in groups, chains and singly, adding a degree of picturesqueness not found in other parts of the Catskill region. Delaware county partakes more of the nature of Greene and Ulster counties; the contour broken and the valleys steep and abrupt, consequently there are few lakes and ponds. Such as there are lie near the Sullivan county line and along the Delaware river. These lakes, mostly fed by springs or streams of spring-water, are eagerly sought by sportsmen, who stock the waters with choice fish. Many of them contain trout and others pickerel, for the preservation of which boards of supervisors have passed laws, but from the fact that there is lacking a strong hand to enforce them they remain inoperative. Many streams and parts of streams in Ulster county are leased from the owners and used as private fishing ground by the parties leasing them.

The forests of the Catskills originally were made up of the same mixture of hard and soft timber as is at present found in undisturbed sections of the Adirondack wilderness: Pine, hemlock, spruce, balsam, maple, birch, beech, ash, oak, hickory, iron-wood, and some elm and poplar. The original pine timber was cut out so many years ago that the memory of the generation of our fathers cannot recall when it was done. No doubt the earliest settlers, away back in the first years of the last century, are responsible for the disappearance of this kind of timber.

In many places there exist at the present day groves of second-growth pine that have sprung up from seed, but the timber is in most cases of an inferior quality and does not make good lumber. It finds a little use in the shape of dock-logs, square sticks of timber used to protect the outer edges of docks and wharves. Many logs when cut will present a fair appearance, with a smooth trunk and clear ends, but when sawed up into lumber

the old knots which have been grown over by the successive annual rings, show themselves, and, as one lumber merchant expressed it, "there are fourteen of 'em to the square foot." Such timber has no market value and it does not pay to grow it. There is some spruce still to be found in the Catskills. A considerable quantity of it is sawed along the headwaters of the Schoharie creek in Greene county; the sawed timber is used in the vicinity of the mills for building purposes and for the manufacture of packing cases, in which articles manufactured from other kinds of timber are shipped to market. There is also a limited supply of hemlock, the greater part of which is in Sullivan county, although there is a small quantity in the towns of Denning and Hardenburgh, Ulster county, which, however, adjoin Sullivan county on the north. The largest part of the supply of tan-bark is shipped from the towns of Sullivan county, and it is on this limited supply that the few tanneries now doing business are dependent. Thirty years ago this Catskill region was in places a dense hemlock wilderness and the business of tanning was the leading industry, at least in Sullivan county and other parts of the Catskill counties, but the avarice of the tanners got ahead of their judgment, and the timber was slaughtered for the bark alone. Many small watermills drove a precarious living on the leavings of the bark-peelers, but the peeling progressed much faster than the sawing, till the woods became filled with the dry trunks and drier tops then the fire caught in these old "peelings," and the old story of total denudation was repeated, perhaps for the first time here, but has been followed up by a repetition every year, with more or less disastrous results. Many localities show these fire-scars; some are recovering, slowly, to be sure, but still a young and hardy timber growth is there, which in time will grow into a tall forest. Some places have never recovered from the effect of the fire and never will, for the soil that sustains the life of the tree has been consumed or washed away. A steep mountain-side once deprived of the mass of clinging roots, moss and leaf-mold, with a network of branches above or a canopy of leaves to break the force of driving rain-storms, is shorn of its power to withstand this force of nature, and the loose masses of loam, sand or other earth overlaying in many instances only to a shallow depth, the smooth faces of the rock, become detached through the action of frost, are washed into the streams threading the valleys below and are carried away to enrich some other section. A thousand years will not re-clothe these denuded mountain-sides with forests, and they are useful for no other purpose. The forests of the Catskills as they now exist are mainly of hardwood, and lacking the appearance of density which a copious sprinkling of evergreens give, they appear thin to the traveler passing through or by them in the winter time, which illusion is somewhat dispelled when the trees are in full leaf.

There are some noble forests crowning the ridges among the headwaters of the Schoharie creek in Greene county, and of the Beaver kill in Ulster county. Mr. S.H. Hine of Cairo, writing in regard to the timber in the mountain regions of Greene county, says:

"The hard timber of our mountains consists of hard maple (curled and birds-eye), rock and white oak, with some red and yellow oak, hickory, white ash, iron wood, beech and black and yellow birch. The largest one variety of hardwood is hard maple, and where it has been left in the virgin state it gives fine specimens. Curled and birds-eye maple have been more eagerly sought for on account of their value for veneering. The soft woods consist of spruce, yellow and white pine, basswood and hemlock, with a large percentage of spruce, which is used for building purposes and in its virgin state shows fine specimens. The reckless waste of mountain forests is plainly visible in this section."

The same remark is applicable to the whole Catskill region, no matter from which side it is viewed, and this is not a thing of the past, nor is the remark to be construed as in the past tense; the "reckless waste" is going on all the time, and the noble forests mowed down to satisfy the cupidity of man, with no thought of replacing them and no provision for their regrowth; in fact the very shoots struggling up at the base of the parent stem possess a marketable value, and scarcely number three years of existence before they are shorn at the root, but so profuse and lavish is nature that another three years sees others as strong and rugged in their place. Some balsam and red cedar are found in the Catskills; there is a stunted growth of the former between Haines's Falls and Tannersville in Greene county. The red-cedar is found nearer the Hudson river on the mountain slopes facing the valley; it possesses little economic value, as the trunks are stunted and curled, and when sawed up the lumber is full of knots. There is a slight consumption of this timber in fence posts, but the supply is nowhere abundant and hence it is of little importance. In Sullivan county and the south-western part of Ulster county bordering on Sullivan, considerable "American laurel" (Kalmia) grows in the woods. It possesses no economic value, however, but is evergreen and hardy and will maintain a foothold where other shrubs would perish. Its presence saves many a mountain side from the appearance of total denudation.

In some of the cloves there can be seen the straight, smooth trunks of the basswood, maintaining foothold among the loose masses of rock and in the shallow soil, their inaccessibility having proved their salvation, as there exists an active demand for this timber

The Downsville flood, April 9, 1895. (Collection of the Delaware County Historical Association)

for the manufacture of excelsior. There is a large consumption all around the whole circumference of this region of nearly all varieties of wood, both hard and soft, and there is no part, except the more remote and inaccessible, but that is called upon to contribute to support, wholly or in part, some industry which means destruction to the forests. With this cutting away of timber there seems to be no provision made for a continuance of the supply, which implies the abandonment at no distant day, of important industries, and the loss to this section of capital and the proceeds of capital. It would be well for the men who conduct these industries to think ahead a little and observe if they can not see the end in the near future, and provide against it in the way that hard experience has taught the people of older nations.

The average quality of the soil of this region is many grades higher than that of the Adirondacks, and those sections which have been cleared up and placed under intelligent cultivation have yielded a fair return. The soil is loamy in the greater number of localities, though there are places where the stones are too thick for the soil to accumulate. Clearings in such places hardly afford poor pasturage and there is no excuse for making them. In referring to this region, the mountainous portions only are meant as the farms along the Hudson river are rich soil and highly cultivated, the peach and grape crops alone grown on them yearly amount in value to hundreds of thousands of dollars. It would be a false economy to advise the reclothing with forests of regions so especially adapted to cultivation as these river farms.

Farming is a family affair, circa 1940s. (Collection of Larry Tompkins)

Agriculture in the mountainous parts occupies, however, a secondary place as a means of gaining a livelihood. The business of entertaining summer boarders from small beginnings has increased to such proportion that the majority of the farmers give up their agriculture and even their homes to care for the seekers after health and recreation.*

The State of New York owns lands in each of the four counties embracing the Catskill region, of the following amounts, viz: Greene county, 661 acres; Ulster county, 32,818 acres; Sullivan county, 576 7/10 acres; and in Delaware county, 12,262 acres, a total of 46,318 7/10 acres. The State lands in three of these counties, viz: Greene, Ulster and Sullivan, constitute and are known as the Catskill Forest Preserve, and are subject to the provisions of the law creating the Forest Commission. Delaware county was excepted, and the State lands within that county are still under the control and management of the Commissioners of the Land Office and the State Comptroller. While this state of affairs exists the people of this county lose the benefit of the act of May 5, 1886, (chapter 280, Laws 1886), which provides for the taxation of State forest lands in the counties embracing the forest preserve. This tax on 12,262 acres would amount to a considerable item and would practically affect those towns where the taxes are felt most burdensome. Also the Forest Commission, through its officers, would throw a protection around those sections particularly exposed to ravages by fire, which could not fail to be productive of good and lasting benefit to the owners of wild and forest lands in this county.

The State's title to the lands in this preserve has come through tax sales by the Comptroller, resale of bonded lands, and bidding in loan mortgage lands. By far the greater amount has been acquired by the State bidding in the parcels at tax sales. In Greene county the titles, with but one exception, were acquired through the Comptroller's tax sales of 1877 and 1881. In Sullivan county, those in the Hardenburgh patent were acquired through the 1871 tax sale, while the remainder of the lands in the Minisink patent were derived severally from mortgage sale, tax sale of 1826 and of 1871, 1877 and 1881.

The title to the State's land in Ulster county has been derived through the county treasurers' tax sales of 1879, 1880, 1881, 1882 and 1883, and the State Comptroller's tax sales of 1871, 1877 and 1881, with a few parcels bid in on mortgage sale. Chapter 260, Laws of 1881, authorizes the sale of lands by the county treasurer for arrears of taxes and legalizes previous sales for taxes made by him. Under this law the county became possessed of a vast amount of wild land, for which there was no market, and from which it derived no benefit, as the lands were untaxed and unproductive of revenue, the county, therefore, found them a dead load on its hands.

*The New York, Ontario and Western Railroad Company estimates that the summer visitors to Sullivan, Ulster and Delaware counties in 1886 expended there a sum equal to four fifths of the total annual value of the farm products of those counties.

Through the enterprise of one or two citizens of Kingston an act was passed repealing the several laws, as far as they affected the county of Ulster, concerning the bidding in of lands by its treasurer, at sales for arrears of taxes, and also authorizing the county treasurer to transfer to the Comptroller all certificates in his possession transferred or issued to the county of Ulster; also legalizing all sales for non-payment of taxes, heretofore made by the Comptroller, whether for the county of Ulster or for the State: also to confirm and make valid the title to said lands, notwithstanding any defects in the assessment thereof, or levying of taxes thereon, unless the title be questioned in a legal proceeding commenced within one year from the passage of the act. This act was passed April 20, 1885, just twenty-five days before the passage of the act creating the Forest Commission. Here, again, is an evidence of forethought and prudence, which from the earliest history of this region has always been justly attributed to the inhabitants of Wildwyk, now the city of Kingston.

The following table shows the distribution of the State lands among the different towns of the three counties, as well as the percentage that the area of State lands bears to the whole area of wild or forest land in the towns.

On the above [see page 169] number of acres of State land in Ulster county, the State paid a tax of $638.25 for the year 1886.*

By glancing at a township map of these counties it will be readily seen that the majority of the parcels in these three counties are situated in widely separated towns, with the exception alone of Hardenburgh and Denning in Ulster county, where a very large body of State land is found, the parcels of which lies in bodies and close together. They are the two wildest and most mountainous towns in the county and with the exception of Shandaken and Wawarsing possess the largest area; they also have the lowest proportional rate of valuation and fewest inhabitants. It is said of Hardenburgh that there is not a liquor saloon or a store in the whole town. In Greene county, the town of Cairo is near the center, while Lexington is near the south-west corner of the county. In Sullivan county, the town of Neversink is in the extreme north-east corner of the county, while Highland and Lumberland border on its southern limit along the Delaware river. This cannot, however, be construed into a disadvantage as it gives a widely extended territory in which the advantages of, and results to be derived from, forest culture, can be better demonstrated to a large number of people.

The means of communication between different sections of this region are very good. Highways for the most part lead from the river, up the valleys of the principal streams and from these other roads find a passage-way across from one valley to another through the numerous "cloves" or notches in the mountain ranges. A network of communication is thus formed, which serves advantageously for getting from place

*No returns were made by the assessors in Greene and Sullivan counties on State lands within their districts.

CATSKILL ACREAGE.

	Area of State Land.	Area of town.	Area of wild or forest land.	Per cent of State lands.
	Greene County. Total Number of Acres, 379,860.			
Town of Cairo	154 acres	35,808 acres	28,646.4	.53
Town of Lexington	507 1/2 acres	47,511 acres	38,009.0	1.33
Total in county	661 1/2 acres	83,319 acres	66,655.4	....
	Sullivan County. Total Number of Acres, 604,705.			
Town of Highland	91 2/3 acres	33, 050 acres	19,830	.46
Town of Neversink	293 acres	45,480 acres	22,740	1.29
Town of Lumberland	191 1/5 acres	32,325 acres	25,860	.73
Total in county	576 7/10 acres	110,855 acres	68,430	....
	Ulster County. Total Number of Acres, 663,331 acres.			
Town of Denning	19,227 4/5 acres	63,668 acres	50,934.4	37.75
Town of Esopus	20 acres	22,247 acres	2,224.7	.90
Town of Gardiner	11 7/10 acres	25,558 acres	2,555.8	.45
Town of Hardenburgh	10,208 acres	53,646 acres	42,916.8	23.78
Town of Hurley	63 acres	20,721 acres	2,072.1	3.06
Town of Kingston	60 acres	4,504 acres	450.4	13.32
Town of Marbletown	27 acres	31,696 acres	3,169.6	.85
Town of Olive	1,747 acres	37,168 acres	7,433.6	23.50
Town of Plattekill	37 acres	20,890 acres	6,267.0	.59
Town of Shandaken	1,115 acres	67,811 acres	33,905.5	3.28
Town of Shawangunk	1/2 acre	35,039 acres	21,023.4	.02
Town of Ulster	10 acres	15,077 acres	1,507.7	.66
Town of Woodstock	131 acres	37,085 acres	14,834.0	.88
Town of Wawarsing	160 acres	73,470 acres	29,388.0	.54
Total in county	32,818 acres	508,600 acres.	218,683.0	....

to place in this region. Other roads have been built along the sides and on the crowns of the ridges, where the wildness of the scenery is the only attraction offered to any one who will risk the fatigue of the climb. Aside from the roads, a perfect maze of paths leads from each of the large summer hotels or places of resort to all the points of interest in which this region abounds. The roads are in some places up very steep mountain sides where the wash from spring rains gulleys them out to such an extent that they are made impassable at times. The soil, however, is very advantageous for road building, and the abundance of flat stones of a large size enables the highway commissioners to thoroughly drain their road beds, which is one of the main requirements in the construction and maintenance of a good road. This same stone also breaks up readily and mixing with good binding earth or clay forms a road bed which in summer becomes as hard as a floor and gives off very little dust. Material of this nature also has great resisting power to the erosive action of water, else these steep mountain roads would be impassable two-thirds of the year.

The discovery of the vast deposits of coal in the Lackawanna beds and the difficulty of floating it down the Delaware river in "arks" to market it, or of carting it or of sledding it over the mountains in small quantities and at great expense, left the owners of these rich mines in such a shape as not to be able to compete with those companies who were flooding a newly created market with coal from other and more accessible regions. This led to the study of the region which formed the natural outlet from the Lackawaxen. The Delaware river had been tried and abandoned as more coal was sunk beneath its waters than was got to market. An examination of the valleys disclosed the fact that a canal could be built from Lackawaxen on the Delaware at the southern end of the town of Highland to Port Jervis at the junction of the Neversink river; thence up the valley of this river to its point of deflection toward the north-west; thence up the valley of the branch joining the main stream at this point, to the summit of the water-shed of the Rondout creek near Wurtsborough, and thence down the Rondout valley to tide water in the Hudson at Rondout. "The scheme of the Delaware and Hudson canal was one of William and Maurice Wurts, of Philadelphia; the survey was made by Benjamin Wright, in 1824, and the estimate cost was $1,300,000; actually constructed it cost considerably more. The canal and railroad were commenced in 1826 and completed in 1828. At first the canal was intended for boats of thirty tons burden; subsequently its capacity was so enlarged as to admit vessels of fifty tons, and finally, improved so as to pass boats of 130 tons." The canal passes through the cement regions about Rosendale, and supplies the means for bringing the coal for burning, and for carrying away the manufactured product. The New York and Erie Railroad, now the New York, Lake Erie and Western, was chartered in 1832. The Legislature appropriated $15,000 to enable Benjamin Wright and his subordinates to examine the route and report the result. His report may be found in the Assembly

Documents of 1835. On the route as reported, the road was not built except that portion of it through the valley of the Delaware river. The railroad enters Sullivan county at Ten Mile river and follows along the banks of the Delaware, passing out at the intersection of the division line between Sullivan and Delaware counties with the river, and thence continues along the river to Deposit, where it passes out of Delaware into Broome county.

The New York and Oswego Midland, now the New York, Ontario and Western, was completed on its present location in 1873. It strikes into Sullivan county near the south-east corner of the extreme eastern part and passes diagonally across the county through the towns of Mamakating, Fallsburgh, Liberty and Rockland, passing into Delaware county at the junction of the Willewemoc with the Beaver kill, thence across the southern end of Delaware county it passes into Chenango county at Sidney.

The New York, West Shore and Buffalo Railroad enters Ulster county at the southeast corner of the town of Marlborough and follows the river through those towns adjacent to it, through Ulster and Greene counties, connecting with the Wallkill valley and the Ulster and Delaware railroads at Kingston, and with the Catskill Mountain Railroad at Catskill. The West Shore and Midland unite at Cornwall in Orange county. The Wallkill Valley Railroad connects Kingston in Ulster county on the line of the West Shore Railroad with Campbell Hall in Orange county on the line of the New York,

Deer hunters in Phoenicia, circa 1920s. (Collection of Town of Shandaken Historical Museum)

Ontario and Western Railroad. It passes through the cement burning region. The Ulster and Delaware Railroad starts at Kingston at the junction of the West Shore with the Wallkill Valley Railroad, and follows the course of the Esopus creek across the northern towns of the county, and thence into Delaware county near the north-east corner of the town of Middletown, thence across this town and the town of Roxbury, and finds a terminus at Hobart, near the center of the town of Stamford. It is a road of heavy grades and sharp curves, but serves as an avenue of approach to those wishing to reach the heart of the Catskills.

From Phoenicia, a station on the Ulster and Delaware Railroad, situated near the north-east corner of the town of Shandaken in Ulster county, a narrow gauge road has been built through the Stony clove across to the valley of the Schoharie creek giving access to the numerous summer resorts at Hunter, Tannersville and landing guests at the Laurel House, Hotel Kaaterskill and the Catskill Mountain House, at an elevation of over 2,200 feet above the Hudson river. This road is operated only from Phoenicia to Hunter during the winter, there being two or three wood working concerns of considerable importance along this portion of the route. The portion not operated through the winter is called the Kaaterskill Railroad.

The Catskill Mountain Railroad connects Catskill village on the line of the West Shore Railroad with Palenville, lying at the foot of the mountain, on the top of which is the Catskill Mountain House. It is a narrow gauge road. There is also a branch to the village of Cairo. The main road was opened in 1882 and the branch in 1885. The main

Successful bear hunters, circa 1920s. (Collection of Lonnie and Peg Gale)

road is entirely within the town of Catskill in Greene county; the branch starts from near the north-west bounds of Catskill, thence to near the center of the town of Cairo.

The Albany and Susquehanna branch of the Delaware and Hudson Canal Company Railroad, follows along the valley of the Susquehanna from its headwaters, skirting the western bounds of Delaware county. In Delaware county there is a branch railroad from Walton, a station on the New York, Ontario and Western Railroad to Delhi; in Sullivan county a branch from Summitville in said county to Ellenville in Ulster county, and another branch from Port Jervis in Orange county, on the line of the New York Lake Erie and Western Railroad to Monticello, the county seat.

The following table [see page 174], compiled from the "Report of the Railroad Commission," will give a fair idea of the magnitude of the railroad interest in the counties embracing the Catskill forest preserve.

The above table shows [see page 174] a large mileage in these four counties. The majority of the railroads run directly through heavily timbered sections, and into these sections particularly are the greatest number of trains run, and in consequence there must be a greater exposure of the woods and waste places to the liability to catch and carry fire from the numerous engines passing over the road. The summer traffic comes in the four driest months of the year, June, July, August and September, when the woods are in the driest condition, and it is at this season that disastrous fires have occurred in the past. During July and August

these pleasure roads in the mountains run from five to eight trains a day each way. This becomes necessary when the vast number of people who visit this region every year is taken into consideration. The New York, Ontario and Western railroad distributes about 25,000 people from their railroad through Sullivan Ulster and Delaware counties. The Catskill Mountain Railroad distributes among the mountain resorts of Greene county about 35,000 people. The Ulster and Delaware Railroad carries into the same section and among the resorts of Ulster and Delaware counties about 35,000 more. Stages and private conveyances carry perhaps 5,000 more, and the New York, Lake Erie and Western leaves 20,000 people to admire the beauties of the Delaware. The total of 120,000 people does not over-estimate the amount of travel to this Catskill region. It is but a hundred miles from New York, Brooklyn and Jersey City, teeming with their millions of population.

This region has not entirely been given over to the interests of the pleasure seeker, though it forms the natural picnic ground of the vast populations of New York and vicinity. For that reason alone, inasmuch as it brings health and vigor to replace wasted vitality to the thousands who seek the pure air of its mountains and the sparkling water of its living springs, part of this region at least should be left in as near a state of nature as at this late day is possible. It is many years ago (nearly half a century) since the Old Mountain House was sought out by the aristocracy of New York and Baltimore, long before railroads were thought of and when

CATSKILL RAILROADS.

County.	Name of railroad.	From—	To—	Gauge. [Ft. in.]	Miles.
Delaware	New York, Ontario and Western	East line of Co.	Sidney	4 8 1/2	62
Delaware	Delhi branch	Walton	Delhi	4 8 1/2	17
Delaware	New York, Lake Erie and Western	East line of Co.	Deposit	4 8 1/2	11
Sullivan	New York, Ontario and Western	East line of Co.	West line of Co.	4 8 1/2	56
Sullivan	Ellenville branch	Summitville	Ellenville	4 8 1/2	8
Sullivan	New York, Lake Erie and Western	Ten Mile River	West line of Co.	4 8 1/2	22
Sullivan	Port Jervis and Monticello	South line of Co.	Monticello	4 8 1/2	12
Ulster	New York, West Shore and Buffalo	South line of Co.	North line of Co.	4 8 1/2	18
Ulster	Wallkill Valley	Kingston	South line. of Co	4 8 1/2	13
Ulster	Ulster and Delaware	Kingston	Hobart	4 8 1/2	27
Ulster	Stony Clove and Catskill Mountain	Phoenicia	Hunter	3 0	6
Greene	Kaaterskill	Kaaterskill Jun.	Catskill M. house	3 0	3
Greene	New York, West Shore and Buffalo	South line of Co.	North line of Co.	4 8 1/2	15
Greene	Catskill Mountain	Catskill	Palenville	3 0	16
Greene	Cairo branch	Junction	Cairo	3 0	4
Total miles					290

the stage coach was the only means of conveyance. Here the great merchants of the one and wealthy planters of the other discussed the political issues of the day on its broad veranda and gathered new life and strength from the invigorating atmosphere, while the wife of the merchant sought to arouse vexation and jealousy in the heart of the wife of the planter by the display of finer tissues of silk and laces and a more liberal supply of jewels. Much the same scenes are still enacted on the same old spot; but there came at times uneasy minds and roving spirits, who explored for the sake of finding something new. Gradually the beauties of this whole region became known, and were written about, till finally every valley, many of the mountains and the desirable places generally became more or less known and finally occupied by a people who make it their business to care for the multitudes who annually swarm to this region for three or four months and leave it desolate for nine.

The fine fishing afforded by the many mountain streams attracts another class of people who come to this region as early as the first of May, but whose stay is very brief. Its proximity to New York makes it an easy matter for the city sportsman to leave business for a few days to angle for the trout in the clear waters of the streams. So common became this practice that the natural increase of the fish could not keep pace with the rate they were taken out, so that artificial stocking of the streams had to be resorted to. Various parties, private individuals and railroad companies have brought thousands of young trout from the artificial hatching

A good day fly-fishing at Cooks Falls on the Beaverkill, early to mid-1900s. (Collection of Delaware County Historical Association)

establishments through the State and have turned the young fry loose among the headwaters of the streams and into some of the lakes and ponds, so that in localities where somewhat protected they now enjoy fine sport, but in the streams where the public is allowed to fish even this liberal supply has proved anything but permanent. Hunting in this region is confined chiefly to grouse, rabbits, squirrels and such small game. Deer are rarely seen and much more rarely killed. The last of the deer were killed off some twelve years ago, when there was a great body of snow fell, on which a crust formed of sufficient strength to bear the weight of a man. Pot-hunters came into this region, presumably from Pennsylvania, and killed large numbers of deer, from which the hides were taken and the carcasses left to rot in the woods. Since that time the hunters have been able to keep pace with the natural increase of the few that were left from the wholesale slaughter. It is fair to suppose that there are not a dozen deer in this whole Catskill region, though the natural features are such as to provide all the requirements for an abundant increase if they were protected and left unmolested to roam the woods at their own sweet will for a few years. In early times the Dutch settler hunted wild turkeys along the beech ridges in the town of Callicoon in Sullivan county; indeed it is said that the name of the town is derived from the sound used by the early hunters in imitation of that bird's note of calling. Be that as it may, there have probably been no wild turkeys in this region or any other part of it for nearly a hundred years, and it is doubtful whether the conditions are such that they could ever be induced to thrive again in the thin, open woods that occupy the places of the then dense forests of that region along the Delaware. There are many miles of streams, the waters of which are leased from the owners by parties residing elsewhere. These waters are kept stocked and to the owners afford fine sport. The same is true of many ponds on whose banks can be seen the club-houses of the owners, who annually repair to the same to enjoy the benefits of out-door life. The cause of the decline in the supply of game and fish in this region is therefore manifest. The cupidity of a few men has caused the deer to become nearly extinct in this region, and the leasing

Tubers on the Esopus Creek. (Mark McCarroll)

of streams has diminished the amount of public waters; consequently those that are left free and open are "fished to death" the first week at the opening of the season and kept in that condition by the army of hungry sportsmen who come later.

It is a matter of great difficulty to tell when the first tanning business was started in this region. The construction of the Delaware and Hudson Canal opened up communication through Sullivan county. This was in 1828, and in 1831 the historian says John Eldridge, Rufus Palen and one or two other large tanners commenced operations here and were followed by other men of their calling, as the bark of Greene, Schoharie and Ulster counties was exhausted. Then Sullivan county became the most important sole-leather manufacturing district in the world. From this it would appear that Greene and Ulster counties were the scenes of the earliest tanning operations.

At Prattsville, on the Schoharie creek, are rocks on which are carvings commemorating the doings of Hon. Zadoc Pratt in this region in years gone by. One is to the effect that 1,000,000 sides of leather were tanned in twenty years with the bark of hemlock cut on the neighboring mountains. Through the Kaaterskill clove are to be seen the ruins of old tanneries and the house of the workmen. Inside the foundation walls of one old tannery are now growing birch trees eight and twelve inches in diameter. The banks of the Schoharie creek from Hunter to Lexington show frequent remains of old tanneries. Manufacturers found it easier to cart the raw materials to the bark than to cart the bark to

the hides, hence the progress has been from Greene to Ulster and thence to Sullivan, from which latter a limited supply of bark is yet to be had. Five years more will witness the last of the tanning with hemlock bark got from this region. So much bark being stripped left a plethora of timber lying in the woods. Some few small saw mills, run by water, were located along the streams, up whose valleys the bark peelers had gone. The owners sought to make a few dollars by sawing up into lumber the immense trunks lying around in profusion, but their mills were of small capacity, and it is safe to say that they did not saw ten feet for every thousand feet that lay in the woods. Old residents say there were never seen such hemlock forests as clothed these mountains, majestic, dark and grand, but that after the bark peelers passed through, millions of feet of the best hemlock timber lay rotting in the woods, and millions more of feet were consumed by the terrific fires which swept through in the way prepared for them. Many claim that if the tanners had never come into this country, these counties would be credited among the richest in the State, instead of being poor and insignificant as they now are. Be that as it may, the hemlock timber is gone, the spruce is practically exhausted, and the determined attack being made on the hard wood will soon witness its extermination also. What then will remain? There are other industries which find a ready use for the young shoots. The prospect, therefore, seems to be that this region is doomed to total and continued denudation, with the exception of the few acres owned by the State, and a few by private individuals, which, under their present management, will be retained as forest land, but under the care of new hands may be devoted to destruction.

Lumbering, except in those sections adjoining the Delaware river, has never seemed to be the industry that it is in the Adirondack region. The rough mountain streams were perhaps not suitable for driving logs. At any rate it does not seem to have been the practice here. The low lands along the Hudson were, at an early day, cleared up for cultivation by the Dutch settlers, at Esopus and Hurley, and by the Huguenots of New Paltz, and history does not give any account of lumbering operations in these localities at any early date. Sullivan and Delaware counties, however, were the scene of quite extensive lumber operations, as, for instance, they have been carried on in the town of Rockland since 1798. Rockland lies in the north-west corner of the county, and is many miles from the Delaware river, but it has within its limits the Willewemoc and Beaver kill, which are tributaries of the east branch of the Delaware. At a much earlier date than that given above, rafting was attempted on the Delaware river with a great or less degree of success. Great rafts of timber bound and locked together would be started down the broad current, poled over the sluggish places and guided over the rifts, sometimes successfully, at other times to go to pieces in a hopeless wreck on some jutting rock when the luckless raftsman counted himself fortunate to escape with his life.

They had their laws, too, these early lumbermen. "In 1791 every non-resident of the town of Mamakating, Sullivan county, rendered himself liable to a fine of 'six pence for every inch across the stump' if caught trespassing by cutting on the timbered lands of another. No exception was made in favor of those who owned real estate in Mamakating but resided elsewhere." Here is an evidence that goes to verify the assertion that a tree in the woods, if of a choice variety as a cherry, curled maple or ash, is considered to be the property of him who discovers it. Timber thieving seems to be a practice sanctioned by the customs of our forefathers, but at the same time was viewed with disapproval by the law-abiding, and also by the owners of desirable standing timber.

Fires have caused much damage through this section, no doubt the railroads are responsible for some of them. But they owe their origin to various causes, which here are very similar to those which give rise to fires in the Adirondack preserve. Berry pickers are here credited with starting many of the fires. The proximity of the New York market and the great demand for the really fine quality of the whortle-berries, which abound on the mountain sides, where for some reason or other the timber has been removed, has caused this class of people to adopt the custom of burning over the fields, with a view of increasing the yield. This is done every year or so, and results in keeping down the young growth of timber which would otherwise spring up in the sufficient soil with which the majority of the mountain sides are covered. The Ellenville Water Works Company suffers from this cause, and a vigorous effort is being made to protect the part of the

Shawangunk mountains occupied by the watershed from which they gather their water supply. It is said that the whortle-berry crop on these mountains, in the neighborhood of Ellenville, is worth from four to five thousand dollars annually, and also that there are houses and lots in the village whose owners have paid for them with money earned by picking berries on the Shawangunk mountains. This is very nice for them, as it amounts almost to a free gift from nature, but it is obtained at the expense of denuding several thousand acres and hindering the timber growth which in time would reclothe this barren ridge with a forest. As has been hinted at, there are many industries located in and about the Catskill mountain region

which are annually making great inroads on the hard wood with which the mountains are thinly covered. Where found the soft varieties suffer also, as there is a ready use found for all. In the first place there is considerable building going on all the time, in the valleys, on the mountains, and everywhere that it is thought an attraction exists to draw the much-prized summer boarder. Farmers who have brought up their families in the little house with one gable tear it down and build in its place a house of many gables. Building, however, is the least harmful of any of the industries. A demand exists in nearly all localities for hemlock and spruce for these operations, and is almost wholly supplied by local saw mills; the pine and finishing lumber

Fishing the Esopus Creek with the Ulster & Delaware Railroad going by, in the late 1930s or early 1940s. (Collection of Roy Winchell)

comes from outside. There is an active demand for bird's-eye maple and for cherry; the former is used in making veneering. Such is the demand for this that the remotest regions are searched, and wherever a tree is found it is taken, regardless of the ownership; the same is true of the cherry. In some sections choice rock maple is sawed into what are called piano-bars. They are made from the best and straightest grained maple, and are two and a half inches by four inches by six feet. The same mills that cut piano-bars also cut what is known as chair stock. This is sawed from almost any kind of hard wood, it not being necessary that the grain should always be straight. Dimensions of stock, two inches by two and a half inches by eighteen inches. In other sections clear straight maple is made into roller-blocks, used in paper mills and calico-print works. These are manufactured and shipped only during the three winter months; the stock is turned up roughly to full six and a quarter inches diameter and twenty-six inches in length. Each roll has to be perfect, with no checks or bad spots. Thirty to forty carloads of these roller-blocks are shipped yearly from Livingston Manor, in Sullivan county. The same firm which ships the roller-blocks manufacture base-ball clubs, Indian clubs and dumb-bells; the two latter are made largely from the cull roller-blocks. The stock for ball bats is two and five-eighths inches square by thirty-five inches to thirty-eight inches long for men's bats, and thirty inches to thirty-two inches for boys' bats. The firm manufactures from twelve to fifteen hundred gross of bats a year, and makes 10,000 pairs of Indian clubs and 25,000 pairs

Hiker signing in at a trailless summit canister. (Chris Olney)

of dumb-bells. Other concerns are engaged in the same line of business. The timber used consists of beech, birch, maple, ash, cherry, and hemlock, the latter used for boxing the manufactured goods. There are several chair factories in the Catskill region, the principal location for the business being in the north part of Ulster county and southern part of Greene. The largest factory of this character is in Stony Clove, at Chichesterville. Here it is said the work is conducted on such a large scale that the green log, fresh from the chipping, is turned in at one end and comes out at the other as one or more finished chairs. Certain it is the log is wholly and completely utilized in one way or another. This concern last year sold 18,000 dozens of chairs, besides thousands of cradles and settees. This factory uses 2,000,000 feet of logs and lumber a year, which comes from the mountains in the immediate vicinity. There are other chair factories at Shandaken, in Ulster county, and at Edgewood and Hunter, in Greene county. Much of the unfinished work is sent to New York.

The wood acid factories, of which there are two in the vicinity of Livingston Manor, consume cordwood at the rate of fifteen to thirty cords of wood a day. Beech timber is considered the best as containing more acid; birch, maple, oak and chestnut are also used. Lime is used in clarifying the acid. The products are wood alcohol, acetate of lime, charcoal, creosote and wood-ashes, all of which have a marketable value. It is said the charcoal alone pays for the raw material and labor. A gas is also generated in the retorts which is utilized in lighting the works which run both night and day.

There are also scoop and bowl makers scattered through the northern section of the town of Rockland, Sullivan county, and the southern part of Hardenburgh, Ulster county. Meat trays are also manufactured. These articles are made from the choice part of the trees, and by a class of poor farmers living in the mountain wooded districts. They find a ready sale, for all they make, at the grocery stores.

Some few oak piles and a little oak ship-timber is cut near Catskill. Other uses to which wood is put in this region, is the manufacture of excelsior from basswood; the manufacture of barrel-hoops from young hard wood saplings; of headings from all kinds of hard and soft wood; of railroad ties (of which there is a large number used annually by the railroad companies whose lines penetrate and cross the region), and last, but by far the greatest use, is in supplying the demand for cord-wood, at the immense brick burning establishments scattered along the Hudson river from Catskill to Croton, the principal of which, however, are at Haverstraw. A few concerns have tried the use of coal, and with good success, but the majority of them prefer to use wood. An immense traffic in this cord-wood has sprung up, brought about by the demand for brick, created by the building of such structures as the Croton Aqueduct, and the unusual activity in the construction of buildings in New York city. Farmers near the river towns finding a ready market for their wood, have cut off many acres of steep hillside adjacent to the river, where the land lies at such a declivity that the cultivation of it is at once out of the question. In this way many beautiful patches of wood which, with other features combined to give to the scenery of the Hudson river its just celebrity, have been laid under contribution, and become denuded slopes, on which it will be many years before a tree growth will again flourish. This wood comes also from along the lines of the various railroads, particularly

Spin firshermen at Junction Pool in Roscoe. (Mark McCarroll)

the New York, Ontario & Western Railroad from Sullivan county.

Some chestnut fence posts are cut in the vicinity of Ellenville and shipped from that place. Also what are called river posts, eight, ten and twelve feet long, used in New York city in cellars, etc.

There has been enumerated the different industries which consume the forest growth of the Catskill region. As regards the distribution of them they are found, in general all around and through this whole section. But particular industries seem to have a somewhat particular locality in which they best flourish.

Turning, including roller-blocks, bats, Indian clubs, dumb-bells, bowls, trays and scoops, as well as the manufacture of wood

acid, is located chiefly in the town of Rockland, Sullivan county, Colchester, Delaware county and Hardenbergh, Ulster county. The manufacture of hoops and headings is in its most flourishing condition in the town of Wawarsing, Ulster county. The great bulk of the hoop-poles comes from the Shawangunk mountains. Ellenville is the market for hoops. They are cut, however, more or less all along the line of the New York, Ogdensburgh and Watertown Railroad. The chair factories are in the town of Shandaken, in Ulster, and in Hunter, in Greene county, which towns adjoin, and the two manufacturing districts are connected by a railroad. The ties are produced in the vicinity of the railroads. Particularly is this true of the Ulster and Delaware Railroad which I am

CATSKILL TIMBER STATISTICS

County	Town	Feet B. M. of timber sawed.	No. of cords of wood cut.	Number of hoops.	Number of rail- road ties.	Feet B. M. of round timber.	No. of acres yearly de-nuded.
Greene	Cairo*	180,000	....	....	....	....	18.0
Greene	Catskill	70,000	2,835	....	....	400,000	223.4
Greene	Hunter	600,000	....	....	....	....	60.0
Greene	Jewett	885,000	600	....	....	....	112.5
Greene	Windham	150,000	....	....	....	....	15.0
Ulster	Denning*	400,000	....	2,000,000	....	....	40.0
Ulster	Hardenbergh*	400,000	....	....	....	....	40.0
Ulster	Marlborough	125,000	....	....	....	....	12.5
Ulster	Olive*	200,000	1,600	....	10,000	....	104.0
Ulster	Saugerties	....	4,500	....	....	....	180.0
Ulster	Shandaken*	3,200,000	....	....	14,200	....	348.0
Ulster	Wawarsing*	1,600,000	12,275	43,000,000	200,000	....	749.3
Ulster	Rondout and Kingston	....	8,800	....	....	....	352.0
Sullivan	Bethel	750,000	....	....	....	....	30.0
Sullivan	Callicon	100,000	....	....	....	....	4.0
Sullivan	Cochecton	200,000	....	....	....	....	8.0
Sullivan	Delaware	850,000	....	....	....	....	34.0
Sullivan	Fallsburgh	75,000	14,250	....	....	....	386.2
Sullivan	Forestburgh	6,050,000	....	....	....	....	242.0
Sullivan	Fremont	300,000	....	....	....	....	12.0
Sullivan	Liberty	575,000	14,250	....	....	....	379.2
Sullivan	Mamakating	....	14,250	10,000,000	....	....	356.2
Sullivan	Neversink*	550,000	....	....	....	....	22.0
Sullivan	Rockland	4,620,000	14,250	100,000	....	50,000	543.0
		21,880,000	87,600	55,100,000	224,200	450,000	2,015.6

*These towns contain lands belonging to the State.

informed will use this year about 24,200, but whether in an extension or repairs was not stated. Excelsior is manufactured at Wawarsing and Boiceville in Ulster. Chair stock is cut in those sections where it can be got by short haul to the railroads, and is sold to local manufacturers or shipped to New York city. The piano bars all go to New York city. Sections of birch trees of large diameter are shipped from Livingston Manor to New York to supply a demand for butchers' blocks. Veneers are cut at Ellenville, chiefly of birch for chair bottoms. For this purpose considerable round timber is shipped by rail to Ellenville, from points west in Delaware and Sullivan counties.

It is a matter of great difficulty to get at anything like the exact amount of timber cut in this region per annum, but a near approximation will be found in the following table [see page 183], with an estimate of the number of acres which would have to be denuded in order to meet this demand. The proportion of cordwood, and feet board measure of timber per acre have been obtained by inquiry in various parts of this region. The majority of men seem agreed that twenty-five cords to the acre of four feet wood is the average yield of Catskill mountain lands, though it has been stated that small parcels have been known to yield forty cords to the acre, but so many agreed on the first figure that this has been assumed as the proper divisor to use. Inquiry also disclosed the fact that the woods are much denser or the timber much larger in some localities than they are in others. For instance in the town of Hardenburgh the figures given were about 4,000 feet board measure, per acre,

for hardwood, while in Hunter, in Greene county, on the opposite side of the valley of the Esopus creek 10,000 feet was given, while in the southern part of the town of Wawarsing, Ulster county, 7,500 feet per acre, and in the town of Rockland in the forest district of Sullivan county, the forests were said to yield 25,000 feet to the acre, which figures perhaps is a trifle high, though the hardwood timber is of enormous size.

The value of the forest lands of the Catskills varies with the location and with the character of the timber growth. Good hoop-pole lands are worth more than heavily timbered lands; those near manufacturing centers, and along lines of railroad, are more valuable than those that are remote from such. The value of such remotely situated lands depends also on the amount of hemlock or spruce on them. In this connection are given some figures at which wild lands are held in various places in the Catskills.

A tract of 500 acres of woodland in the town of Hunter, Greene county, it is said, could be bought for one dollar and fifty cents per acre, exclusive of the spruce timber which would be reserved. In Stony Clove, town of Hunter, standing timber is valued at fifty cents to two dollars per thousand feet, which would make timber lands about there worth from fifteen dollars to twenty dollars an acre.

Timber lands in the town of Rockland, Sullivan county, are held at four dollars to ten dollars an acre, depending on their location, soil and timber. Two hundred acres in Rockland were sold recently at twelve dollars an acre. The land had a fair cut of hemlock timber on it.

The following information has been gleaned in making a tour of the counties embracing the Catskill forest preserve and will show the opinions of the people on the various matters under discussion.

Two thousand acres in the town of Shandaken, Ulster county, are held at four dollars per acre. Lands in the town of Denning are held at two dollars to ten dollars per acre. Six hundred acres of land from which the hemlock alone had been removed, located in the town of Denning, were recently sold for one dollar and a half an acre. A citizen of Ellenville, who owns 1,500 acres in the town of Wawarsing, will sell at two dollars and a half per acre. Hoop-pole lands near Ellenville, if good, are worth from ten dollars to twenty-five dollars per acre.

Hon. Thomas Cornell owns a controlling interest in the Ulster and Delaware Railroad, running from Kingston in Ulster county to Hobart in Delaware county. The road derives its income from the large amount of freight carried to and from the manufacturing towns in the interior of the county, and also from summer tourists who are attracted by the scenery, mountain air and fishing along the line of the road. The company has spent large sums of money every year stocking the streams with trout fry. Mr. Cornell owns Furlough Lake in the town of Hardenburgh, the waters of which flow into Dry brook and thence to the Delaware. If any stealing of timber takes place in that vicinity, it will be probably on the lots in the Connecticut Tract, in Great Lot 6, of the Hardenburgh Patent, in the town of Hardenburgh, and the timber stolen will be all hard wood, as maple and birch, and would be taken out to the line of the New York, Ogdensburgh and Watertown Railroad and shipped away. It is stated that the railroad would require this year about 24,490 ties, and that they had carried out to the West Shore Railroad 1,350 cords of wood all coming from the interior towns along the line of the road.

Canoeing on the East Branch of the Delaware River. (Chris Olney)

THE BRICK INDUSTRY

An acquaintance with one of the owners of a large brick kiln, brought out some facts in relation to this industry which have a very pertinent bearing on the subject of forest growth. Eight brick yards at Rondout and vicinity use over 8,000 cords of wood. A good portion of it is drawn in by farmers coming from within a distance of fifteen miles of the yards. A large quantity comes from Shandaken on the Ulster and Delaware Railroad. Mountain lands will cut twenty-five to thirty cords to the acre. The ruling prices have been this winter four dollars and fifty cents to five dollars and twenty-five cents per cord. From five to six cords are burned to every 42,000 brick; it takes less wood when the bricks are well dried, and more when business is rushed and the bricks burned wet. There was a brick yard at Kingston as early as 1695, which furnished the first brick used in Kingston.

Another brick-maker at Catskill furnished the following information; Of 500 cords of wood used by him a year, mostly hard wood, at least three-fourths comes from the town of Catskill; the ruling price this year has been four dollars and seventy-five cents per cord. Other concerns about there use over 2,000 cords annually; 300 cords are shipped from there to other places along the river. A yard between Saugerties and Rondout uses more wood than all the brick-yards in Catskill together. Two concerns at Glasco must use 1,000 cords. Another, six miles below, uses 500 cords a year. They own 200 acres of woodland in the town of Athens and cut therefrom an average yield of twenty-five cords of wood to the acre. Fifty acres are hemlock and pine. The remainder is oak, some chestnut and a large quantity of red-cedar. Brick-makers are beginning to use coal instead of wood, but few yards, however, try it. There are a few thousand feet of oak ship-timber and some oak piles sold here and some pine too knotty for lumber is used for dock-logs. Fifteen million brick are made at Catskill a year. At Cornwall from five to ten car loads of cord-wood are shipped daily to the brick-yards down the river. It all comes from Sullivan county by way of the New York, Ohio and Western Railroad. On the nineteenth of March there were forty car loads standing on the side track at Cornwall. The wood is shipped in five car lots. Between Kingston and Cornwall there has been much clearing up of the steep hillsides close to the river; the wood being cut up in to four feet lengths and shipped by the railroad. A resident of the town of Wawarsing, in Ulster county, says 50,000 cords will about represent the amount of cord-wood shipped out of Sullivan county by way of the New York, Ohio and Western Railroad, and the Delaware and Hudson canal; the railroad carrying about two-fifths of the amount. It goes, most of it, to Haverstraw. There is a great quantity of cord-wood piled at many places along the line of the Delaware and Hudson canal ready to be shipped as soon as the canal opens for navigation.

VARIOUS INDUSTRIES. — *By County*

Delaware County.

Griffin's Corners.— One mill run by water power.

Arkville.— Is the shipping point for chair stock cut by mills up the Dry Brook valley in the town of Hardenburgh, Ulster county.

Greene County.

Catskill.—This is the starting point of the Catskill Mountain Railroad, fifteen and three-quarter miles in length; connects Catskill with Palenville at the foot of the mountain. The road is narrow gauge (three feet). It has a branch to Cairo, three and three-quarter miles long, operated for summer traffic only, in June, July, August and September. Through the summer months it carries about 35,000 people. During July and August seven trains each way are run on the main line and eight on the branch. In the spring and fall three trains are run each way. The road was opened in 1882; the branch in 1885. The summer freight business is about one-eighth of the passenger traffic. About one-half the travel goes to Cairo, and one-half to the Mountain House and Palenville. Fifteen hundred acres around the Mountain House are owned by Mr. Beach. The face of the mountain below the hotel has been stripped of its original growth and is now grown up with a thin covering of birch, oak, poplar and white birch. No cutting of timber is done on the hotel lands.

At *Palenville* is a small saw-mill run by water power from the Kaaterskill creek, capacity 1,000 feet a day of boards, or 2,000 feet of lumber; saws both hemlock and oak. Hemlock lumber is worth sixteen dollars a thousand and oak forty dollars. The mill supplies only a local market, the proprietor owns no woodland; but buys his stock from farmers; he runs a tannery in connection with the mill but has done nothing for the past three years, owing to the low price of leather. There is no bark to be had in the neighborhood.

Good ice-fishing at Big Pond. (Chris Olney)

Haines's Falls.—From Palenville the road follows up through the Kaaterskill Clove, a narrow gorge with high steep mountains on either side. On the north side the mountain is steep, precipitous and rocky, scantily covered with a growth of small trees, as scrubby pines, some cedar and hemlock. To the south the land rises more gradually and has a heavy timber growth, mostly large trees of the hard wood varieties, among which is a fair sprinkling of hemlock and on the tops of the highest ridges is a good growth of fair sized spruce. This valley was cut over by the tanning companies about thirty years ago, and from Palenville to the foot of the mountain are to be seen occasionally the remains of the tanneries and the dwelling-houses of the workmen.

Haines's Corners.—From this place the grade is downward and the water now flows to the Schoharie creek. There is a small saw-mill here of about 2,000 feet daily capacity.

Tannersville, lies partly on the highway and partly on the railroad, the two parts being separated about half a mile. North from the upper portion is a wide stretch of flat country, mostly a farming section, with a few houses. A cluster of large hotels is here for the accommodation of summer boarders. There is a steam mill in the woods working out chair stock.

Clum Hill, across the valley from Tannersville, was burned over some years ago and is now covered with a fine growth of young trees. Many thousand California trout have been put in the streams which here form the headwaters of the Schoharie creek. The board of supervisors have passed a law pro-

The Catskills are well known among ice climbers. (Mark McCarroll)

hibiting fishing in the stocked streams for two years.

Hunter.— A chair factory here consumes about 125 to 150 thousand feet of lumber of year. One saw-mill cuts about 2,000 feet of lumber a day, mostly spruce. Another, a steam-mill, two miles above towards Stony Clove is the principal mill for building lumber about here; rough lumber is worth about fifteen dollars a thousand. The tops of the mountains here are all more or less covered with spruce, while the sides and valleys are grown up with maple and hard wood a limited quantity of ash and cherry. The valley was originally covered with pine, above the hemlock and hard wood, and on top of the ridges the spruce. In 1857 fire ran through these parts; poplar sprung up after the burning and is now used for manufacturing excelsior. Seventy to eighty car loads were sent out from here last winter.

An old resident of Hunter says: "Thirty years ago there was a heavy growth of hemlock on these mountains. Twenty-five years ago tanning was the leading industry. Twenty years ago the hemlock became exhausted. Nothing has been done here in that line for fifteen years. There were two large tanneries and two small ones in this vicinity. The working up of the hemlock timber into lumber did not then pay expenses. Very little of the money that was made out of the tanning business staid [sic] here. The tanneries left us poor." He sold the poplar on two hundred acres at two dollars an acre for the standing timber; it yielded four cords to the acre. Some of the land about here has become valuable as a source of spruce lumber. Building is active in this vicinity. A tract of five hundred acres below here, known as the McKivver tract could be bought at $1.50 per acre, exclusive of the spruce timber. The chair factory at Edgewood buys all the logs that can be got from the farmers. The other establishment located below the village does the same. Some logs come from the town of Jewett adjoining Hunter. The price is ten dollars a thousand in the log, and for sawed ash lumber twenty dollars a thousand is paid when delivered at the factory. Six or seven public houses here accommodate from 100 to 150 people each. There are besides a number of families that keep a few boarders during the season.

Lexington.— There is no manufacturing done here; the only business is caring for summer boarders and farming. The Schoharie creek is still-water in front of the village. Thirty years ago there were tanneries in this vicinity, but they were conducted by outside capital, and the money made from the business went away and did the locality no permanent good. Poplar has come up in the old peelings and is now fair sized.

Westkill.— On the branch of the Schoharie, of that name, is a small settlement of houses and summer hotels. Passing south on the highway to Shandaken through the clove the summit is reached about a mile from Westkill village. The mountain sides are very steep, but thickly covered with a good growth of fair sized timber, very little of which is of any evergreen variety. There is considerable basswood of medium size. Beyond the summit the water runs south, heading in a small pool. No agricultural lands are met until Bushnellville is reached, and here they constitute merely a small strip along the creek bottom, mostly dairy farms. Some timber is cut and drawn to the chair factory at Shandaken.

Bushnellville.— Originally supported a tanning business, a chair factory and a spring-bed-bottom factory, basswood being used in the latter industry; the factories were run until the timber was all cut out. Business stopped some twenty-five or thirty years ago. The mountain sides for a long distance around are now sparsely covered with a thin growth of small stuff.

Edgewood.— A chair factory on the Stony Clove creek, about four miles above

Chichesterville, consumes from 1,000,000 to 1,200,000 feet of lumber a year. There are, perhaps, a million or two feet of standing spruce timber on the ridge between the Schoharie and Esopus creeks. This mill only manufactures "in shape," the material goes to Hunter where it is finished and set up. The price paid here is seven dollars per thousand for timber in the log. The company have about one million feet of logs now in the yard.

Orange County.

Middletown Tannery.— Has an annual capacity of 1,800 tons of bark, the principal part of which comes from Sullivan county; a small part, however, comes from Delaware county. Bark costs seven dollars unloaded on cars. This tannery has been in operation twenty-one years. From Ellenville to Eureka the road is through the valley of the Rondout creek.

Sullivan County.

At *Eureka.*— The east branch of the Rondout creek joins the main stream. Much of the water of this branch is leased for fishing purposes by non-residents, who have their notices up at frequent intervals along the stream forbidding parties from trespassing on their rights. The valley at all places is narrow and contracted and the hills steep on either side. They are now sparsely covered with a thin growth of saplings, among which old stumps can be seen, giving evidence of a once heavy growth of timber on these hill-

sides. This valley is said to have been once a great place for hemlock, but the bark peelers came along slaughtering the timber for the bark faster than the small water-mills could cut it up, consequently millions of feet went to waste, rotting in the woods, then the fire came and swept through, burning the dead and fallen timber, and with them the woody portion of the soil, so that the future growth of forests was sadly interrupted.

Livingston Manor.— There is located here a wood-alcohol and acetate of lime factory, which has been running seven years. It has twelve retorts and two condensers, and consumes 3,000 cords of hard-wood per year. Beech is considered the best for the purpose, but there is used also birch, maple, oak and chestnut. The products of the factory are wood-alcohol, acetate of lime, creosote and wood ashes. This alcohol is used in varnishes; the acetate of lime is used by white lead manufacturers and in dyeing; the charcoal is used by powder manufacturers and the wood ashes are used as a fertilizer. The alcohol is worth two and one-half cents a pound, and the capacity of the works is one barrel a day. Fourteen cords of wood are consumed in producing it. Parties running it pay two dollars a cord for wood delivered in the factory yard, and buy of farmers living in the vicinity. There is another factory five miles up the Willewemoc, which has sixteen retorts and has been running five years. It consumes 4,000 cords of wood a year. At each burning the Livingston Manor factory use fourteen cords of wood. The retorts are filled once in twenty-four hours. The company has to carry a year's stock of wood. A gas which is generated in the retorts is used to light the factory nights. The charcoal sells for thirty-seven and one-half cents a sack, which contains four bushels. The charcoal pays for the wood and for the labor. The ashes from under the retorts are worth twelve cents a bushel. In Delaware county, just west of the Sullivan county line, there are located a large number of these wood-acid factories. These are at East Branch, Fish's Eddy, Trout Brook, Westfield, Reed's Creek and Rock Rift. The wood supply for these comes all from Delaware county. Scoop and bowl makers are scattered through the upper part of the town of Rockland, Sullivan county. They also make the oblong butcher's trays. These articles are made from the choice part of the tree, by a class of poor farmers living in the mountain-wooded districts. Trays are sixteen, twenty and twenty-four inches long; scoops are worth about four dollars and fifty cents per dozen. The manufacturers trade them at the store for groceries and necessaries. There are several small turning establishments near the north line of the county, where the trays are made by machinery. There are five of these mills on the Beaver kill and its tributary, Shin Creek, and two on the Willewemoc. These will produce two hundred to five hundred dozen each a year; total yearly product, about 2,000 dozen. A twelve-foot log, nineteen inches in diameter, will make one and one-half dozen trays. A merchant says: "We handle about 40,000 hoops and buy some trays, bowls and scoops. We take them in trade. I bought, individually, 200 acres of timber land in the town of Rockland, from which I peeled 660 tons of hemlock bark. I paid twelve dollars an acre for the land. There is a basket factory in the town of Marlborough, which uses 120 to 125 thousand feet of selected birch a year, shipped mostly from here. There is a tannery at Rockland using 1,200 cords of bark a year, and is the only one in the town of Rockland. Tanning has all been abandoned here within ten years. The largest and next to the largest were abandoned during the last two years."

Halls Mills covered bridge on the Neversink River. (Chris Olney)

Volunteer trail work is a great way to give something back for our natural resources. (Chris Olney)

The turning shop at Livingston Manor manufactures baseball bats, Indian clubs, dumb-bells and everything in the wood turning line. Bats, clubs and dumb-bells are the main product. There is used, all told, about 800,000 feet in turning these articles; this includes 100,000 feet of ash, with the prospect of using more of this timber from now on, and are gradually working into that alone. There is also used about 50,000 feet of basswood, the balance of the amount is birch, beech, maple and some cherry, of the latter say 25,000 feet. The timber all comes from within a couple of miles of the factory, except the ash which is got all along the line of the railroad where it can be picked up. They ship a great many roller-blocks, for paper rolls, to England. These are all hard maple, six and one-fourth inches in diameter when turned and twenty-six inches in length. All stock of this kind has to be perfect and free from checks and bad spots. They ship from thirty to forty car loads a year, during the three cold months; they cannot ship in warm weather as the timber checks under the influence of the heat. They cut most of their beech, birch and maple lumber from the log, and pay five dollars a thousand for logs delivered in the yard. Standing timber on the lands about here is worth from one dollar and fifty cents to two dollars and fifty cents a thousand feet, board measure, and timber lands are said to be worth from four dollars to ten dollars an acre. There is another shop of the same character at Westfield, about six miles below here, with about the same consumption of timber as this. The factory here manufactures 1,200 to 1,500 gross of bats, 10,000 pair of Indian clubs, and 25,000 pair of dumb-bells a year. Stock for bats is two and five-eighths inches square by thirty-five to thirty-eight inches long for men's sizes and thirty to thirty-two inches long for boy's sizes. They use cull roller blocks for making Indian clubs and dumb bells. The proprietors of the factory own three hundred acres of standing timber; in cutting it off his lands he clears everything. Stock is cut down to ten inches on the stump and what is left from this, is cut up into cord-wood; the price paid here is two dollars and twenty-five cents a cord delivered on cars. Good timber land, if cut for cord-wood alone, will average forty cords to the acre. The proprietor of the shop thinks they can run on the present supply of timber about fifteen years longer; they have already been here fifteen years; they used to buy timber for four dollars a thousand, but since for the last five years they have been clearing the timber up so fast the price has risen. For the last three years dealers have started shipping out round timber and cord-wood and are increasing their business every year. They use in the turning shop from 100,000 to 107,000 feet a year of hemlock for boxing goods which is worth from nine dollars to ten dollars a thousand, and has been as high as twelve dollars. They use three turbine wheels, a twenty-four, thirty-six and forty inch, working on a nine foot head of water obtained from Willewemoc creek.

A timber and wood dealer says that 50,000 cords will about represent the amount of cord wood shipped out of this country by way of the New York, Ontario and Western Railroad, and by the Delaware and Hudson Canal, and that of this amount the railroad carries about two-fifths. Most all of it goes to Haverstraw to supply the immense brick burning establishments.

Acid Factories.— The Middletown Argus says: "The decline of the lumber business along the line of the Ontario and Western Railroad in Sullivan and Delaware counties was followed by the introduction of a new business, which was intended to utilize the hard wood forests which clothed many of the hills and mountains after the supply of hemlock had been exhausted. This new business was the establishment of factories for the manufacture of pyroligneous acid or wood acid, and what is called in commerce, acetate of lime. The acetate is produced by the destructive distillation of wood in closed retorts, and the incidental products of its manufacture are wood-alcohol and charcoal. The pioneers in the business made large profits, for the demand for their products exceeded the supply, but it was not long before there were so many engaged in the business that the market was overstocked, and the prices declined to a point below the cost of manufacture. The result was, of course, that many factories shut down. About two years ago the market for the products of these factories began to improve, and the improvement has continued ever since, until now prices for acetate and alcohol are more than double what they were two years ago. At present prices the business affords a good profit, and if the present conditions continue, good times for the owners of the factories will mean increased activity and employment for woodchoppers and others dependent upon them for employment."

Ulster County.

Shandaken.— Is on the Ulster and Delaware Railroad. A chair factory, about a mile below the station, on the north side of the Esopus creek, consumes about 500,000 feet of hard wood timber a year.

Chichesterville.—The Chichester Chair Company is located here on the Stony Clove creek. It uses 2,000,000 feet of logs and lumber annually, at a cost of $2,400; will use probably more than that this year. All kinds of hard wood are used, also spruce and hemlock for packing cases. The company owns about 5,000 acres of woodland in Woodstock and Shandaken, Ulster county, and Hunter and Lexington in Greene. It cuts timber down to eight inches on the stump and estimates the yield at 10,000 feet, board measure, to the acre. It has very little trouble from fires. Eight or nine years ago two serious fires occurred, which, however, were controlled, but not until serious damage had been done and the factory and buildings threatened. Timber costs six dollars a thousand cut on their own lands and seven dollars a thousand if there is not one hundred feet in the log, and eight dollars if there is.

The refuse from the factories is burned under the boilers and no coal is used. The company had rather buy the logs than the sawed lumber, as it can get the slab from the former which is good turning stock. It pays ten dollars a thousand for green lumber and twelve dollars for dry. Standing timber is appraised at one dollar and fifty cents to two dollars per thousand. Dry ash lumber is worth twenty dollars per thousand. The company realized last year $900 in rentals from bluestone quarries. It clears some land for hay and cut enough last year to supply its

Bald eagle fledglings — a species making a comeback in the Catskills. (Scott VanArsdale, NYSDEC)

needs. It buys timber rather than use its own; which it reserves against a rise in the market. It makes finished chairs, cradles and settees. A great proportion of the work goes to South America, Cuba and Panama. Since being in business here the water-power has failed wonderfully; formerly it used water-power alone, now it uses part steam. Mr. Chichester planted about one-fourth of an acre two years ago with black walnuts; the young trees are now about five feet high and one inch in diameter, and healthy looking; they grow rapidly. A stream coming down from the west has its water-shed now grown up pretty well with small stuff, and the summer flow of this stream is greater than that of the main stream, of which it is a tributary. On the main creek the floods are often violent and disastrous and are believed to result from cutting off the timber on the steep hillsides of the valley. Twenty-five years ago, rough stock only was manufactured and carted to Rondout. The railroad had not then been built.

Phoenicia.— Two mills run by water-power.

Fox Hollow.—One mill run by water-power. Blue stone piled ready for shipping.

Shandaken.—A chair factory.

Big Indian.— One mill run by water-power.

Pine Hill.— One mill run by water-power.

Summit Station.— Two charcoal pits, not now in use.

Dry Brook.— Is the name of a section of country and not of a village. The brook is a rapid stream occupying a narrow valley between steep hills. There are four saw-mills on this stream, two run by water power and two by steam. These mills saw some hemlock of which there is a small amount left in remote localities, but saw mostly hard wood for chair stock and piano bars, which find a fair market along the Ulster and Delaware Railroad. The State lands in this vicinity are reached from the Dry Brook road; they are covered with a thin growth of hard wood, with an occasional clump of hemlock; some of the maple and birch is very large and of fine quality. The lots lie, for the most part, on the tops and further sides of the ridges, and aside from an occasional cherry or ash tree stolen, are unmolested. The Quaker Clearing near Balsam Lake, covers about 1,000 acres. It has been used as pasturage for stock, but is unoccupied at present. There originally stood an old forge about four miles up from the mouth of the brook. Charcoal was burned many years ago in that locality; it is not known where the ore came from.

Piano-bars are made from the best and straightest grained maple, and are cut two and one-half inches by four inches, by six feet in length. Chair stock is cut from almost any kind of hard wood and it is not necessary that the grain should always be straight; birch, as well as maple, is sawed for this; the dimensions of stock are two inches by two and one-half inches, by eighteen inches long. All the poplar has been cut out of this valley and used in the manufacture of excelsior.

Mount Pleasant.— Has two saw-mills run by water power; railroad ties and hoops shipped from here.

Boiceville.—Has one saw-mill run by

water power; railroad ties and cord wood shipped from here.

Shokan.— One saw-mill run by steam; one tannery and one set (3) of charcoal pits; railroad ties are shipped from here.

Broadhead's Bridge.—Has one mill for sawing bluestone; railroad ties, mostly chestnut, and considerable cord wood are shipped from here.

West Hurley.—Has one steam mill for sawing bluestone.

Ellenville.—From Kingston to Ellenville, by way of Cornwall, the distance is about eighty-four miles, while by the stage route up the valley of the Rondout creek the distance is only about twenty-eight miles. There has been talk of building a railroad through this valley, which would certainly prove a great saving both of time and money to the people of Ellenville in going to and from Kingston, the county seat. A resident of this place says he owns 3,000 acres of land in the town of Wawarsing in a solid chunk; he is much troubled with persons who burn over his land in order to promote the growth of whortleberries with which they abound, and hopes the State will be able to stop this evil as his lands are about ruined.

A local surveyor says that the 160 acres owned by the State in Great Lot 24 of the Rochester Patent lies on the side of the Shawangunk mountains, about two miles down the Sandberg from here. The land has some good pine sawing timber on it, but most of the hoop-pole stuff has been stolen off. The lot is not near any road.

A lumber merchant says: "We handle three or four million feet of lumber a year, the great majority of which comes from Sullivan county; the shipping points are Rockland and Livingston Manor. The lumber is mostly hemlock, with some maple and chestnut; we handle some pine, cherry and ash; we will handle this year, perhaps, 200,000 feet; hemlock lumber costs eleven dollars on cars; maple, fifteen to twenty dollars; chestnut costs eighteen dollars; cherry, twenty-five dollars; pine, twenty dollars and basswood eighteen dollars. The pine is of an inferior quality, having about thirteen knots to the square foot. The whortleberry crop on the Shawangunk mountains amounts to $4,000 a year, gathered within three or four miles of this place. These pickers burn over the mountain every year in some portion of it to improve the yield. The berries go to New York by rail, sometimes three carloads a day; they are shipped in one-half bushel boxes."

The Ellenville glass-works use from 1,000 to 2,000 cords of wood a year; most of it comes from Greenfield and Oak Ridge or within a radius of about eight miles from here, all from this county and town of Wawarsing; none comes by rail, as the supply can be kept up from what is drawn in by farmers and offered for sale; the price paid is three dollars a cord for hard wood; some hemlock is bought, but mostly hard wood is issued. The material for the glass is a silicious rock, containing about ninety per cent of pure silica; it is dug on the Shawangunk mountains, opposite here, and crushed in the factory; a twenty horse-power engine will crush eighteen tons of the rock a day. Another company has been formed here which will sell the powdered rock to glass

The balance of man and nature manifested in the Catskill Park. (Mark McCarroll)

companies. They claim to have discovered a bed of rock which analyzes 99.63 per cent of pure silica, and are putting up a plant to crush the rock.

Another lumber merchant says: "We handle on an average 1,000,000 feet of hemlock a year, three-fourths of which comes from Parksville, Livingston Manor and Rockland, in Sullivan county, and the balance from Albany; we have also been getting a small percentage from Pennsylvania. We handle 1,000,000 feet of pine, all coming from outside places, as Oswego, Albany and Michigan. Also 50,000 feet of Georgia pine, 50,000 feet of white-wood, 1,000,000 lath, mostly from Glens Falls and Pennsylvania; 2,225,000 shingles, largely from Oswego. We merely handle sawed lumber and do no manufacturing. We manufacture, four miles below here, at Wawarsing, about 50,000

bushels a year of lime for fertilizing and tanners' use. We own six acres of stone quarry within a short carting distance of our two kilns, of a capacity each of 100 bushels of unslacked lime a day."

One of a firm which deals in wood ash said: "We handle about 9,100 cords of wood, which comes from Wurtsborough, Brownsville, Westbrookville and Summitville, in Sullivan county; we pay about three dollars per cord. We handle 200,000 railroad ties, and pay thirty cents for good and half-price for seconds. We handle 500,000 feet of chestnut fence-posts; also a limited number of river posts, cut eight, ten and twelve feet in length, the price of which is one cent per foot; they are used in New York for cellars; only chestnut timber is used. We handle 1,000,000 hoops; we own a mill at Livingston Manor, of about 6,000 to 8,000 feet per day capacity."

Ellenville Pottery.—"This concern uses 250 to 275 cords of wood a year; it is all soft wood, as hemlock and pine, and is cut within a radius of ten miles around here; farmers bring in two, three, four or five cords a piece; the price paid is two dollars a cord."

A hoop dealer says: "Hoop makers begin to shave about the first of October and quit the first of April. The timber used for hoops consist of chestnut, rock oak (red) soft maple, birch, hickory, white oak, black ash and quite a good deal of willow, and is cut in lengths from four and a half to eight feet; the principal part are six and half feet in length, and is all small second growth, one and a half to three-fourths inches in diameter. A large portion of the hoops sold here comes from the town of Wawarsing. Hoop-pole stuff grows up in three or four years, that is, lands cut over reproduce a new crop in from three to four years. I will handle about half a million hoops this year. I own lot 131 in town of Denning, near Parksville." Lands in Denning are held at from two dollars to ten dollars per acre.

Another hoop dealer says: "The hoop-pole range takes in about from here to Allegerville, and includes both sides of the mountains for a distance of sixteen miles, this territory will produce about 45,000,000 of hoops a year from Ulster and about 10,000,000 from Sullivan county. The Shawangunk mountain produces about two-thirds of the Ulster output. The Sullivan county output comes from Wurtsborough. I will get 2,000,000 hoops this year from Claryville in the town of Denning, Ulster county. Denning produces, of all kinds, about two or two and one-half millions a year, all of which go to the Burden Iron and Steel Works at Troy and are used on horse-shoe kegs. The cement manufacturers made 2,250,000 barrels of cement last year and you can count twelve hoops used on each barrel. The staves for these barrels come from the east. Headings come from here, near Wawarsing, and are made of all kinds of tim-

Enjoying the hidden country lanes of the Catskills. (Mark McCarroll)

ber, both hard and soft. The number of headings are two to each barrel and there are three pieces to each head, the dimensions of which are five-eighths inches thick by eighteen inches square, worth four cents a set. Heading stuff is cut square and turned up to sixteen inches diameter. The farmers about here think as much of their hoop-pole lots as they do of their grain fields. I have known of twenty-five to thirty hoop-poles to grow from one chestnut stump. Timber when cut low down gives a far better yield of stump shoots. Hoop-pole lands, if good, are worth from ten dollars to twenty-five dollars per acre; that depends on the situation and soil. Scrub oak is not fit for hoop-poles. Where a soil produces chestnut, maple, or oak, it is more valuable for hoop-pole growing than for agriculture. Such lands will sell, in cases, for more than the timber is worth. Ten years ago last summer I was the first to handle hoop-poles in this locality, and have averaged from that time five to ten million hoops a year. Another dealer has handled a similar number for the same period. Another has handled two million a year. Two others each one and one-half million a year for the last ten years. A New York party has handled five million a year for the last five years. Another three million a year. The bulk of this output comes from the Shawangunk mountains. The hoop-pole industry will produce more money than the whole grain crop of Ulster county. Hoops are bought by the thousand, and the average price for the last ten years has been about four dollars per thousand for all kinds. Headings are sawed in this town (Wawarsing) and in the town of

Rochester; the bulk of them come from Rochester. Headings are sold by the set; the average price for ten years has been four and one-half cents a set."

A mill owner says: "I own a lot in Greenfield and am cutting it off this year: the lot contains fifty-six acres and will yield about 400,000 feet of timber. On the Willowemoc lands, in Sullivan county, the average cut of beech, birch and maple will be 25,000 feet per acre. Veneer stock comes from Sullivan county and is measured by the square foot when cut up into chair-bottom sizes, and is sold by the thousand square feet. The average price for the past year has been twenty shillings per thousand. The ratio of veneer to logs is fifteen thousand feet of veneer to one thousand feet in the log. The capacity of my mill is one hundred to one hundred and fifty feet of logs. The market is in New York and I ship from here by rail. I think private lands could be bought for twenty shillings an acre. I own fifteen hundred acres which I would sell at the above figures."

Ellenville Tanning Company. — Annual capacity is 2,000 cords of bark; supply comes from Delaware county, principally from the town of Hancock. The company run another tannery at Wawarsing of a capacity of about 1,500 tons of bark a year. The supply for this tannery comes from the town of Denning, Ulster county. Bark is worth five dollars and fifty cents and is bought by the ton; some extract is used. The state land can be bought at one dollar and fifty cents per acre. This company sold, recently, 600 acres in Denning at the above figure.

At Napanock.— There is an ax factory, tobacco-knife factory, straw-paper mill and rake factory. The latter concern buys oak in the log and saw and season themselves. The oak is cut in the immediate vicinity and drawn in by the farmers. There are four other mills between Napanock and Eureka, on the Rondout creek, all small saw-mills run by water power, each of about 100,000 feet capacity a year, but are run only part of the time and supply merely a local demand.

Lackawack.— Has a small excelsior mill, using about 500 cords of wood a year. The merchantable timber here is mostly chestnut, which is sawed chiefly into railroad ties and shipped out to the places along the canal and railroad.

Wawarsing. — A manufacturer says: "I use water power in my mill from eight to nine months of the year. Previous to 1863, I used water power entirely, but since then have been obliged to use steam part of the year. The water power is derived from the Vernooy kill which heads a little north-east of lot 1 in the Pell tract. I use 800 cords of wood a year, some of which comes from Neversink, Sullivan county, and some from Wawarsing and Rochester in Ulster. I pay five dollars for 144 cord feet. The wood is cut four feet six inches in length. I buy down to three and one-half inches diameter, and cut down to five inches diameter on the stump. Eight or nine cords of wood make a car load. I own 12,000 acres of timber land, and the timber on other tracts; 1,600 acres of this is in the Pell tract and some in Vernooy's survey. I have another mill at Boiceville, Ulster county, and consume there 1,600 cords of wood a year; my land is located in the town of Shandaken, Ulster county, and in the town of Andes, Delaware county, about one and one-half miles from Andes village. I can furnish the number of all lots owned. Lands from which the timber has been cut off, as a rule, are not used for agriculture, but are allowed to grow up again and then cut over for hoop-poles. This practice keeps the water-sheds in a denuded condition and spoils the water supply."

The industries of Ulster county were never more flourishing than they have been the past year, with a prospect for as busy a season the ensuing year. The largest of these are blue-stone, brick, cement and lime. To these may be added the hoop, heading and cord-wood productions. The hoops and headings are used by the cement and lime manufacturers. About 30,000,000 hoops are used in these two branches alone in this county. This great number of hoops is mostly gathered, prepared and taken to market in the fall and winter when other work is scarce. The cord-wood is used principally by the brickmakers, some of whom use from 4,000 to 5,000 cords in a season. These several items make a tremendous business.

There are other industries in this county. At Ellenville there are glass works and a large leather manufacturing establishment; at Napancock are two paper mills and an axe factory; at Mill Hook, in Rochester, is a paper mill, and in Rochester all the mill-stones to grind the cement and lime are made; in Marbletown near Stone Ridge is a paper mill; in Saugerties a paper mill, turning out ten tons of white paper a day; at Wallkill, town of Shawangunk, a paper mill making two tons of white paper a day. In Olive there are excelsior, pulp and leather manufactories. In Shandaken there are two chair factories, where the logs are rolled in at one end of the establishment, and chairs, cradles and settees come out at the other at the rate of one a minute. At Marlborough there is a berry crate and basket manufactory for shipping fruit to market. Ulster county is likewise a great fruit-raising county, not to mention the immense proportions of the summer boarding business.

There is rarely found in the Catskill region an abandoned homestead, which in itself is good evidence that a continuous cultivation does not exhaust the soil, and that the farms are productive enough of wealth to enable the farmers to purchase the necessary fertilizers. This distinguishes this wild region from the similar one in the Adirondacks, where deserted homesteads are met at frequent intervals, and in places the dilapidated remains of whole villages, which for some reason or other were abandoned many years ago. The Catskill region as a whole has a good soil and friendly climate, which the Adirondacks can scarcely be said to possess. 🖋

CHARLES F. CARPENTER

Tent camping in the Peekamoose Valley. (Mark McCarroll)

Appendix B
Catskill Park Metes-and-Bounds Description

The "Catskill park" shall include all lands located in the counties of Greene, Delaware, Ulster and Sullivan within the following described boundaries, to wit: Beginning in Ulster county at the intersection of the easterly line of the Hardenburgh Patent with the southerly bounds of the Rondout Reservoir; thence running southwesterly along the easterly line of Great Lot 4 of the Hardenburgh Patent to the southeasterly corner of lot one of the East Allotment,

Hunter Mountain fire tower and cabin. (Chris Olney)

east division of Great Lot 4; thence northwesterly along the southerly bounds of lots one, 7, 8, 14, 17, 22, 26, 33, 37 and 46 of said East Allotment, east division of Great Lot 4 and along the southerly bounds of lots 67, 49, 48, 47, 46, 45, 44, 43, 42 and 41 of the Middle Allotment, east division of Great Lot 4 to the center of the Neversink creek; thence northerly along the center of the Neversink creek to the southeasterly corner of lot 37 of the West Allotment, east division of Great Lot 4; thence northwesterly along the southerly bounds of lots 37, 27, 22, 11 and 6 of said West Allotment, east division of Great Lot 4 to a point in the easterly line of the town of Rockland in Sullivan county; thence southerly along the easterly line of the town of Rockland in Sullivan county to the northeasterly corner of the town of Liberty; thence northwesterly along the northerly line of the town of Liberty in Sullivan county to the southwesterly corner of lot 120 of the East Allotment, middle division of Great Lot 4; thence northwesterly along the southerly bounds of lots 119 and 118 of the East Allotment, middle division of Great Lot 4 to a point in the center of the Willowemoc creek; thence westerly down the center of the Willowemoc creek to its confluence with the Beaver Kill; thence northwesterly down the center of said Beaver Kill to the southwesterly line of the town of Colchester in Delaware county; thence northwesterly along said southwesterly line of the town of Colchester in

Delaware county to the westerly bank of the east branch of the Delaware river; thence along the westerly bank of the said east branch of the Delaware river and the westerly bounds of the Pepacton reservoir to its intersection with the mouth of the Bush Kill at or near the village of Arkville; thence up along the center of said Bush Kill to the New York Central Railroad; thence along the said New York Central Railroad easterly to the line between the counties of Delaware and Ulster; thence northeasterly along that line to the southerly line of Greene county; thence northwesterly along the southerly line of Greene county to the southwesterly corner of Great Lot No. 21, Hardenburgh Patent; thence northeasterly along the westerly line of said Great Lot No. 21, Hardenburgh Patent to the south bank of the Batavia Kill; thence along the southerly bank of the Batavia Kill easterly to the west line of the State Land Tract; thence northerly, easterly and southerly along the line of the said State Land Tract to the line of the Hardenburgh Patent; thence easterly and southerly along the general easterly line of the Hardenburgh Patent to the southwest corner of the town of Saugerties in Ulster county; thence easterly along the southerly line of the town of Saugerties to the westerly bounds of the New York State Thruway;

thence southerly along the westerly bounds of the said New York State Thruway to the northerly bounds of the Esopus creek; thence in a general westerly direction up and along the northerly bounds of said Esopus creek to its intersection with the southwesterly line of the town of Ulster; thence northwesterly to the southwest corner of the Hurley Patentee Woods Allotment; thence in a general southwesterly direction along the southeasterly line of the Hurley Patentee Woods Allotment to the northerly line of the town of Marbletown; thence northwesterly along said northerly line of the town of Marbletown to the town of Olive; thence southwesterly along the line between the towns of Olive and Marbletown to the line of the town of Rochester; thence northwesterly along the line between the towns of Olive and Rochester to the point where the Mettacahonts creek crosses the same flowing easterly; thence southwesterly parallel with the northwesterly line of the town of Rochester to the southerly bounds of the Rondout creek; thence westerly along the southerly bounds of the Rondout creek and the southerly bounds of the Rondout Reservoir to the easterly line of the Hardenburgh Patent, the point or place of beginning.

Index

Adirondack Council, 134
Adirondack forest preserve, 32, 33, 52, 64
  access, 62
  constitutional protection of (1894), 18, 20, 54-55
  created (1885), 18, 41
  criteria for land acquisitions, 63, 65
  definition, 16, 41, 44
  early example of conservation, 20
  fifty-year anniversary (1935), 66
  funding for purchase of lands, 49, 62, 65
  highway in, 65
  original acreage, 44
  ownership pattern, 49-50
  purpose of, 19
  recommended by Forestry Commission, 36-37
  stone, sand, and gravel for highway purposes, 65
  wilderness lands within, 18, 51, 62, 75
Adirondack Mountain Club, 61, 90, 134
Adirondack Mountains, 28, 31, 33, 34, 35, 44, 48
Adirondack Park, 16, 20, 48, 49, 57
  Alvord bill to create (1874), 35
  blue line defining outbounds of, 50, 68
  boundary of, 20, 61
  created (1892), 51
  defined, 51, 61-62
  land acquisitions within, 65, 66
  private lands in, 57, 58, 62
  recommended by Forest Commission, 51
  State Land Master Plan, 75
Adirondack Park Agency, 62
  created (1971), 75
Albany, city of, 47, 53
Albany Evening Journal, 31
Albany Institute, 33
Allegany River, 34
Altona, town of (Clinton County), 44
Alvord, Thomas (Assemblyman)
  Adirondack Park bill (1874), 35
American Revolution. *See* Revolutionary War
Andes, town of (Delaware County), 72
  forest preserve acreage in (1888), 48
  included in Catskill Park (1904), 59
  Little Pond Campground, 75
Anne, Queen (of England).
  See Queen Anne
Appalachian Mountain Club, 90
Ashland, town of (Greene County)
  included in Catskill Park (1904), 59
Ashokan Reservoir, 69, 72, 79, 87
Association for the Protection of the Adirondacks, 62, 63, 134, 146
Atlantic Ocean, 46
Balsam Lake Club (1883), 32, 61
  lands added to Catskill forest preserve, 80-81
Balsam Lake Mountain (Ulster County), 24
  fire tower, 24, 61

Basselin, Theodore B.
  appointed to Forest Commission, 44
Bearpen Mountain (Greene County), 77
Beaverkill Association, also Beaverkill Trout Club (1875), 32
Beaverkill Campsite, 65
Beaverkill Club (1878), 32
Beaverkill Conservation Area, 80
Beaverkill River, Valley, and Range, 72, 80-81
Belleayre Mountain (Ulster County)
  fire tower, 61
  forest preserve lands on, 64
  Ski Center, 67
Binnewater Class, Kingston Commons, 69
Blackhead Mountain (Greene County), 64
Bond Acts
  of 1916, 62, 64
  of 1924, 65
  of 1960-62, 73-74
  of 1972, 79-82
  of 1986, 84
  of 1993, 84
  of 1996, 85
Brooklyn, city of, 40, 51
Brooklyn Constitution Club, 53
Burroughs, John (naturalist), 32
Bushnellsville, hamlet of (Ulster-Greene counties), 79
Buttermilk Falls, 79
Cairo, town of (Greene County), 70
  forest preserve acreage in (1885), 45
  included in Catskill Park (1904), 59
campsites or campgrounds. *See* public campsites
Capital Region (New York State), 22, 28
Carpenter, Charles R., 20
  inspector, Forest Commission, 47
  report of, 47-48
Catlin, George (artist), 31
Catskill "Blue Line", The, 57
Catskill Center for Conservation and Development, The, 86, 134, 137, 139-140
  Balsam Lake Club, 80-81
  Catskill Park study and recommendations, 7
  founded (1969), 76
Catskill forest preserve, 17, 22, 25, 28, 32, 51, 54, 55
  access, 62, 88
  additions under 1972 bond act, 81-82
  additions under 1986 bond act, 84
  additions under 1993 and 1996 bond acts, 84-86
  area, 17, 59
  area (1885), 25, 44, 45
  composition, 17
  constitutional protection of (1894), 18, 20, 54-55
  created (1885), 18, 41
  criteria for land acquisitions for, 63, 65
  deer parks authorized in, 56
  defined, 16, 41, 44

early example of conservation, 20
ecosystems and habitats, 17
features of, 46
fifty-year anniversary (1935), 66
forest types, 25
land classification, 129-132
management of, 18, 90-94, 129-134
master plan, 91, 93, 94, 129-132
ownership pattern, 49-50
purchase of land for, 49, 52, 56, 59, 61, 63, 65, 73-74, 81-86
purpose of, 19
stone, sand, and gravel for highway purposes, 65
taxation of lands of, 47
unit management plans, 132-133
wilderness lands within, 18, 23, 25, 62, 74, 75, 77
Catskill Mountain House, 65, 83
  burned by state, 83
Catskill Mountains, 16, 33, 35, 70, 72
  as source of water supply, 23
  forest destruction in, 36
  forest soils in, 36, 48
  forest types within, 25
  forests of, 36
  inspection of, by Charles Carpenter, 47-48
  painters of, 30
Catskill Park, 16, 25, 28, 51, 56
  area, 17, 59, 60, 71, 78-79
  blue line defining outbounds of, 50, 59, 68, 70
  boundary established (1904), 20, 59
  businesses within, 22
  counties within, 17, 59
  defined, 20, 61-62, 92
  expansion of, 61, 68-72
  forest preserve lands outside, 61
  forest preserve lands within, 61
  land acquisitions within, 17, 59-60, 66-67
  natural and man-made features within, 21, 22, 46
  New York City Watershed within, 21
  private lands within, 17, 21, 22, 26, 61, 135-140
  proposed, 58-59
  proposed expansion, 77
  public lands within, 17, 21, 22,, 26, 61, 90-94, 129-134
  purpose of, 19, 57
  recreational opportunities within, 22
  State Land Master Plan (1985), 91, 93-94, 129-132
  tourism industry, 22
  wildlife within, 21
Catskill 3500 Club, 90, 134
Catskill, town of (Greene County), 70, 72
  included in Catskill Park (1904), 59
Catskill, village of, 68
Cauterskill. *See* Kaaterskill
Chapin, Alfred C.
  assemblyman, 40

comptroller of New York State, 36-41
  mayor, city of Brooklyn, 40
  Speaker of Assembly, 40
charcoal industry, 29, 36
Civilian Conservation Corps, 65
Cleveland, Grover (Governor)
  message of 1883, 35
Clinton County, 34, 35, 44
Colchester, town of (Delaware County), 69, 72, 79
  forest preserve acreage in (1888), 48
  included in Catskill Park (1904), 59
Cole, Thomas (artist), 30
Colgate Estate and Lake, 80
Colvin, Verplanck
  climbs Mount Seward, 33
  "father" of Adirondack forest preserve, 44
  quoted, 33, 48
  report to New York State Museum of Natural History, 33, 48
Commission of Fisheries
  created (1868), 32
Commission of State Parks, 48
  established (1872), 34, 35
  report of (1873), 34
Committee on State Forest Preservation, 53
comptroller of New York State, 35, 36, 47
  battles with Cornelius Hardenbergh, 38-41, 44, 56
  taxation of lands in Ulster County, 38-41, 44, 56
Conservation Commission, 62, 63, 66
Conservation Department, 38, 41, 57, 66, 67, 68-71, 78
Constitutional Convention
  of 1894, 53-55, 62
  of 1915, 62
  of 1938, 62
  of 1967, 62, 75
Cooper, James Fenimore (novelist), 31
Cornell, Alonzo (Governor)
  message of 1882, 35
Cox, Townsend, 52
  appointed to Forest Commission, 44
  climbs Slide Mountain, 46-47
Croghan, hamlet of (Lewis County), 44
Crown of England, 28
Cuomo, Mario (Governor), 84
De Tocqueville, Alexis
  quoted, 29
Dannemora
  town of (Clinton County), 44
  prison, 44
Dawson, George (editorialist), 31
deer parks, 56
Delaware Bay, 46
Delaware County, 17, 46, 60, 69
  added to forest preserve, 48
  Catskill Park within, 17, 59, 70, 72, 79
  deer parks authorized in, 56
  forest preserve acreage in, 48, 72
  funding for purchase of lands in, 51
  industries in, 47

visited by Forestry Commission, 36
Delaware-Highlands Land
   Conservancy, 139
Delaware River, 46, 69
   East Branch of, 46, 48, 72
Denning, town of (Ulster County)
   county-owned lands in, 56
   forest preserve acreage in (1885), 46
   included in Catskill Park (1904), 59
   lands purchased for forest preserve
     in, 56
detached parcels, 16, 70
   constitutional amendments, 67-68
Devil's Tombstone Campsite, 65
Doubletop Mountain (Ulster
   County), 80
Durham, town of (Greene County)
   included in Catskill Park (1904), 59
Durham Valley Land Trust, 139
East Kill Valley, 80
Ellenville, village of (Ulster County), 47
Emerson, Ralph Waldo (essayist), 31
Erie Canal, 33, 46
Esopus Creek and Valley, 46, 60, 64,
   67, 69, 80
Essex County, 34, 35, 49, 51
Evers, Alf (Catskills historian)
   quoted, 21
Fenwick Lumber Company, 25
fire towers
   Balsam Lake Mountain, 24, 61
   Belleayre Mountain, 61
   Hunter Mountain, 61
   Overlook Mountain, 67
   Red Hill, 65
   Slide Mountain, 61
   Tremper Mountain, 65
fish and fishing, 30, 32, 46, 50
Fisheries Commission, 55
Fisheries, Game, and Forest
   Commission, 55, 56, 57, 58
Flower, Roswell (Governor), 51, 52
   quoted, 52
Fly Fishers Club of Brooklyn (1895), 32
Forest Commission, 47, 48, 51, 52,
   55, 58
   commissioners appointed, 44
   duties and responsibilities, 41, 48
   established (1885), 41
   report of 1890, 49
   report of 1891, 51
   staff of, 47
forest fires, 29, 34, 36
Forest, Fish, and Game Commission,
   58, 60, 62, 78
Forest Preserve Board
   report of 1900, 57
Forest Preserve Expansion Fund, 68
forests
   Adirondack, 17, 33
   Catskill, 17, 36-37
   preservation of, 45, 50, 53, 54
Forestry Commission
   funded (1884), 35
   report of (1885), 36-37
Fox, William F.
   assistant warden,
     Forest Commission, 47

Francis, Austin (author, historian)
   Catskill Rivers, 32
Franklin County, 34, 35, 49, 51
Fulton County, 35
Game Commission, 55
game, fish and. *See* wildlife
Garmon, Samuel F.
   warden, Forest Commission, 47
Giant Ledge (Ulster County), 24
Glen Cove (Long Island), 44
Goodelle, William
   delegate, 1894 Constitutional
     Convention, 53
Graham Mountain (Ulster County), 80
Great Lakes, 34
Greene County, 17, 60
   Catskill Park within, 17, 59, 72, 79
   deer parks authorized in, 56
   forest preserve within, 44, 45, 70
   funding for land acquisition in, 51
Grinnell, George Bird
   editor, *Forest and Stream,* 32
Halcott, town of (Greene County),
   70, 72, 77, 79
Hamilton County, 34, 35, 49, 51
Hammond, S. J. (author)
   quoted, 31
   Wild Northern Scenes (1857), 31
Hancock, town of (Delaware
   County), 69, 72
Hardenbergh, Cornelius, A. J.
   assemblyman, 40, 44
   battles with comptroller, 38-41, 44, 56
   early years, 38
   "father" of Catskill forest preserve, 44
   opposition to taxes, 38
Hardenbergh, Johannes, 28
Hardenbergh (or Hardenburgh)
   Patent (1708), 28, 69
Hardenburgh, town of (Ulster
   County)
   county-owned lands in, 56
   forest preserve acreage in (1885), 46
   included in Catskill Park (1904), 59
   lands purchased for forest preserve
     in, 56, 60
   Little Pond Campground, 75
Harriman, Averell (Governor)
   quoted, 71
Hasbrouck, Gilbert D. B.
   assemblyman, 40
Herkimer County, 34, 35, 51
Highland, town of (Sullivan County)
   forest preserve acreage in (1885), 45
High Peaks Region (Adirondacks), 49
Hill, David B.
   governor, 41
   message of 1890, 49
*Historical Background, Catskill Forest
   Preserve* (1973), 57
Hogan, Michael
   forester, Forest Commission, 47
Hough, Franklin B., 33
   chief, Federal Division of Forestry, 32
   doctor, 32
   historian, 32
Hudson River and Hudson River
   Valley, 22, 34, 46, 51
Hudson River School of Landscape
   Painting, 30, 31

Hunter Mountain (Greene County)
   fire tower, 61
   forest preserve lands on, 64
   lumbering on, 25
Hunter, town of (Greene County)
   Colgate property, 80
   Devil's Tombstone Campsite, 65
   included in Catskill Park (1904), 59
   North Lake Campsite, 65
Hurley, town of (Ulster County), 70, 72
Husted, James W.
   assemblyman, 41
Indian Head Mountain (Greene
   County), 80
Ingham, Charles Cromwell
   founder, National Academy of
     Design, 30
   painting, *The Great Adirondack
     Pass,* 30
Ives, Garry
   chief of Bureau of Preserve
     Protection and Management
     (NYSDEC), 21
   quoted, 21
Jewett, town of (Greene County)
   Colgate property, 80
   included in Catskill Park (1904), 59
Joint Legislative Committee on
   Natural Resources, 57, 67, 77
   Catskill Park expansion, 68-72
   detached parcels study, 68
   park boundary study, 68-70
Kaaterskill Clove, 64, 70
Kaaterskill High Peak, 64
Kings County, 40
Kingston, city of, 40, 47, 68, 77
Kingston Commons, 69
Kingston, town of (Ulster County),
   70, 72
Knevals, Sherman W.
   appointed to Forest Commission, 44
Kudish, Michael (historian), 25
Lake George, 35
   islands in, 35
land conservation organizations
   various, 85-86
land maps
   Adirondack, 57
   Catskill (1899), 56-57
Lands and Forests, Division of
   (NYSDEC), 57, 70
Laws
   Act of Attainder (1779), 28
   of 1872, Chapter 848, 34
   of 1876, Chapter 297, 35
   of 1879, Chapters 200 & 371, 38
   of 1879, Chapter 382, 39
   of 1880, Chapter 573, 39
   of 1881, Chapter 260, 39
   of 1881, Chapter 402, 39
   of 1883, Chapters 13 & 470, 35
   of 1883, Chapter 516, 40
   of 1884, Chapter 551, 35
   of 1885, Chapters 158 & 283, 40-41
   of 1886, Chapter 280, 44
   of 1887, Chapter 475, 48, 51, 52
   of 1888, Chapter 520, 48
   of 1890, Chapters 8 & 37, 49
   of 1892, Chapters 356 & 707, 51-52

   of 1893, Chapter 726, 52
   of 1897, Chapter 259, 56
   of 1899, Chapter 521, 56
   of 1900, Chapters 20 & 607, 56
   of 1904, Chapters 233 & 717, 59
   of 1912, Chapter 444, 61
   of 1916, Chapter 569, 62
   of 1921, Chapter 401, 65
   of 1924, Chapter 275, 65
   of 1929, Chapter 195, 66
   of 1957, Chapter 787, 70
   of 1960, Chapters 522, 523 & 759, 73
   of 1967, Chapter 665, 74
   of 1969, Chapter 1052, 75
   of 1976, Chapter 455, 68
Leopold, Aldo (naturalist), 18
Lewis County, 32, 34, 35, 47, 53
Lexington, town of (Greene County),
   70, 77
   forest preserve acreage in (1885), 45
   included in Catskill Park (1904), 59
Liberty, town of (Sullivan County), 69
Little Pond Campground (Delaware
   and Ulster counties), 75
logging industry, 28, 29, 31, 34, 36,
   44, 62
Long Island, 44
Low, Henry R. (Senator), 41
Lowville, hamlet of (Lewis County), 47
lumbering. *See* logging industry
Lumberland, town of (Sullivan
   County)
   forest preserve acreage in (1885), 45
MacKaye, Benton (preservationist), 18
Macomb, Alexander
   purchase of state-owned land
     (1792), 28
Manufacturer's Aid Association of
   Watertown, 32
Marsh, George Perkins (author), 31
   Man and Nature, 31
Marshall, Louis (conservationist), 62
Marshall, Robert (wilderness advo-
   cate), 18, 19, 62
McClure, David
   chairman, Committee on State
     Forest Preservation, 53
   quoted, 54-55
Mereness, Charles
   delegate, 1894 Constitutional
     Convention, 53
Middletown, town of (Delaware
   County), 70, 72
   forest preserve acreage in (1888), 48
   included in Catskill Park (1904), 59
Middletown, village of (Orange
   County), 41, 68
Milmoe, Wheeler (Senator)
   chairman, Joint Legislative
     Committee on Natural
     Resources, 70
mining industry, 34
Mongaup Pond (Sullivan County), 67
   campground, 75
mountains and mountain peaks. *See*
under specific mountains
Mount Seward, 33
Muir, John (conservationist), 32
National Park Service (1916), 18

National Wilderness Preservation System, 19
Nature Conservancy, The, 83, 86, 134, 139
Neversink River, 46, 67
Neversink, town of (Sullivan County),
  forest preserve acreage in (1885), 45
  included in Catskill Park (1904), 59
New Jersey, northern, 22
New York Board of Trade and Transportation, 53
New York City, 22, 40, 44, 51, 65
  water supply system and reservoirs, 67
  watershed, 21, 86-87
New York City Department of Environmental Protection (NYCDEP), 86-87, 143
New York/New Jersey Trail Conference, 90, 134
New York State, 28, 32
New York State Constitution, 17, 54-55, 58
  amendments of 1913-1953, 62
  amendment of 1931, 66
  amendment of 1947, 67
  amendment of 1987, 67
  Article VII (1894), 55, 67
  Article XIV (1938), 67, 91-92
  defines forest preserve, 17
  detached parcel amendments, 67-68
  proposed amendment 1895-96, 55-56
  proposed amendment 1904-07, 59
  proposed amendment 1932, 66
  protection of forest preserve (1894), 18, 20
New York State Department of Environmental Conservation (NYS-DEC), 16
  Bureau of Preserve Protection and Management, 21
  created (1970), 75
  Division of Lands and Forests, 57, 70
  lands managed by, 16, 18
  management of forest preserve, 18
New York State Legislature, 34
New York State Museum of Natural History, 33, 48
New York State Office of Mental Retardation and Developmental Disabilities, 80
New York State Office of Parks, Recreation, and Historic Preservation (NYSOPRHP), 16
  formerly Council of Parks and Outdoor Recreation, 74
  lands managed by, 16
  park regions of, 74-75
New York State Thruway, 69
New York Times, 31, 48
North Lake, 65, 70
  additions to campsite, 83-84
  campsite, 65
  renamed North Lake-South Lake Campground, 83
Odell, Benjamin (Governor)
  message of 1902, 58
  message of 1904, 58
  quoted, 58
Olive, town of (Ulster County), 70, 72

included in Catskill Park (1904), 59
Oliverea, hamlet of (Ulster County), 60
Olmsted, Frederick Law (landscape architect), 32
Oneida County, 49
Oneonta, city of (Otsego County), 68
Open Space Institute, 86, 139
Open Space Plan, 84
Orange County, 38, 41, 47
outdoor recreation. See recreation
Overlook Mountain (Ulster County)
  fire tower, 67
Palenville, hamlet of (Greene County), 70
paper industry, 29
paths. See trails and paths
Peekamoose Valley (Ulster County), 24, 46, 79
Peekskill, city of, 41
Pennsylvania, state of, 69
Pepacton Reservoir, 72, 79
Pine Bush, hamlet of (Orange County), 38, 41
Plateau Mountain (Greene County), 64
Platte Clove, 64
Pomeroy, Robert Watson (Assemblyman)
  member, Joint Legislative Committee on Natural Resources, 70
Port Jervis, village of (Orange County), 46
Prattsville, town of (Greene County)
  included in Catskill Park (1904), 59
public campsites
  Beaverkill, 65
  Devil's Tombstone, 65
  Little Pond, 75
  Mongaup Pond, 75
  North Lake-South Lake, 65, 83-84
  Woodland Valley, 65
Queen Anne (of England), 28
railroads, 28, 30, 34, 36, 50
Raymond, Henry J. (editorialist)
  quoted, 31, 48
recreation, outdoor, 66, 72, 84, 90
Red Hill (Ulster County)
  fire tower, 65
reforestation, 66
reforestation areas, 66
  on forest preserve lands, 56
Revolutionary War, 28, 34
Rochester, town of (Ulster County)
  included in Catskill Park (1904), 59
Rockefeller, Nelson (Governor), 72, 73
Rockland, town of (Sullivan County), 69, 72
  Beaverkill Campsite, 65
  included in Catskill Park (1904), 59
  Mongaup Pond Campground, 75
Rondout-Esopus Land Conservancy, 139
Rondout Reservoir, 72, 79
Roosevelt, Franklin D., 61
  president, 66
Roosevelt, Theodore (Assemblyman)
  quoted, 36
St. Lawrence County, 34, 35, 51
St. Lawrence River, 34

Salmo Fontinalis Club (1873), 32
Saratoga County, 35
Saratoga Lake, 30
Sargent, Charles Sprague
  Forestry Commission, 36
  professor, Harvard University, 36
Saugerties, town of (Ulster County), 69
  included in Catskill Park (1904), 59
Saugerties, village of (Ulster County), 46
Schoharie Creek, 46, 64
Shandaken, town of (Ulster County)
  Belleayre Ski Area, 67
  county-owned lands in, 56
  forest preserve acreage in (1885), 46
  included in Catskill Park (1904), 59
  Woodland Valley Campsite, 65
Sharpe, George H.
  assemblyman, 40
  Speaker of Assembly, 40
Shawangunk, town of (Ulster County), 70
Shawangunk Kill, 38
signboard law, 75
Slide Mountain (Ulster County), 46, 60, 90
  climbed by Forest Commissioner Cox (1886), 47
  deer park on, 56
  fire tower on, 61
  funding for survey of forest preserve on, 52
  public path to summit authorized (1892), 52
South Lake Campground. See North Lake
Special Committee of the Senate on the Future Policy of the State in Relation to the Adirondacks and Forest Preservation
  Catskill Park proposed by, 58-59
  report of 1904, 58-59
Stony Clove (Greene County), 24, 60, 64, 65
Stony Hollow (Ulster County), 77
Sugarloaf Mountain (Greene County), 64
Sullivan County, 17, 60, 69
  Catskill Park within, 17, 59, 70, 72, 79
  deer parks authorized in, 56
  forest preserve within, 44, 45, 72
  funding for acquisition of lands in, 51
  Mongaup Pond acquisition, 67
Syracuse, city of, 53
tanning industry, 28, 34
Temporary State Commission to Study the Catskills
  created (1971), 76
  extent of study area, 76
  membership, 76
  recommendations, 76-77
  support members, 76
Thomas Cole Mountain (Greene County), 64
Thoreau, Henry David (essayist), 31
trails and paths, 52, 65, 90-91
Train, Abner L.
  secretary, Forest Commission, 47
Tremper Mountain (Ulster County)
  fire tower, 65

forest preserve lands on, 64
Tuscarora Club (1901), 32
Twin Mountain (Greene County), 64
Ulster County, 17, 38, 47, 52, 60
  board of supervisors, 39
  Catskill Park within, 17, 59, 72, 79
  deer parks within, 56
  forest preserve within, 44, 46, 70
  funding for purchase of lands in, 51
  lands owned by, 56
  taxation of forest preserve lands in, 47
  taxation of lands owned by, 38, 44, 56
  treasurer of, 39
  visited by Forestry Commission, 36
Ulster, town of (Ulster County), 70, 72
United States Forest Service (1905), 18
Van Put, Ed (author, historian)
  The Beaverkill, 32
Vesell, Elliot (historian)
  quoted, 30, 31
Vly Mountain (Greene County), 77
Warren County, 35, 51
Washington County, 37
Watershed Agricultural Council, 139
water supply, 31, 45, 50
  of Albany, 33, 34
  of New York City, 21, 33, 65, 67, 86-87
  reservoirs on forest preserve lands, 62
waterways, rivers, lakes, etc. See under specific names
Wawarsing, town of (Ulster County), 70, 72
  included in Catskill Park (1904), 59
West Kill Mountain (Greene County), 24
  forest preserve lands on, 64
  wilderness area, 79
Whitman, Walt (poet), 31
Wild, Peter (author), 31
  quoted, 32, 33
Wilderness Act, National (1964), 18-19
  author of (See Zahniser, Howard), 19
Wilderness Society, 19
wildlife, 30, 50, 56
Wildwyk (early name of Kingston), 47
Willowemoc Club (1868), 32
Willowemoc Stream, 72
Windham, town of (Greene County)
  included in Catskill Park (1904), 59
Woodland Valley Campsite (Ulster County), 65
Woodpecker Ridge, 80
Woodstock Land Conservancy, 86, 139
Woodstock, town of (Ulster County), 70, 72
  included in Catskill Park (1904), 59
Woodstock, village of (Ulster County), 67
Yellowstone National Park (1872), 18
Yosemite Valley (California), 18
Zahniser, Howard, 19
  as Adirondack resident, 19
  author of National Wilderness Act, 19
  quoted, 19, 25

About the Authors

Norman J. Van Valkenburgh

Born in West Kill in the heart of the Catskill Mountains, Norm Van Valkenburgh is the recognized historic authority on New York State's Forest Preserve in the Catskills and Adirondacks. Van Valkenburgh's professional career was devoted to the New York State Department of Environmental Conservation, where he worked from 1955 until his retirement in 1986. At the department Van Valkenburgh began as a land surveyor, then joined the Bureau of Land Acquisition at the Albany headquarters in 1961. He served as chief of the Bureau of Land Acquisition from 1973 to 1976, regional director of the NYSDEC office in New Paltz from 1976 to 1978, and finally as director of the NYSDEC Division of Lands and Forests in Albany from 1978 to 1986. Thousands of acres of forest preserve and other categories of public land in the state were acquired for the public trust under Van Valkenburgh's supervision; a truly lasting legacy for the people of New York. Today Van Valkenburgh works part-time for the Mohonk Preserve on title and land surveying issues on the Shawangunk Ridge. He and his wife Dorothy live in Saugerties, NY.

Among Van Valkenburgh's other books are *Old Stone Walls* (Purple Mountain Press, 2004), *The Adirondack Forest Preserve* (The Adirondack Museum, 1979), *Land Acquisition for New York State: A Historical Perspective* (The Catskill Center, 1985), *New York State Forest Preserve Centennial Fact Book* (NYSDEC, 1985), and the *Murder in the Catskills* series (Purple Mountain Press, 1992, 1994, 1998, 1999). Van Valkenburgh co-authored with Al Forsyth the booklet *The Forest and the Law II*, and is the editor of Verplanck Colvin's *1898 Report of the Superintendent of the State Land Survey* (Association for the Protection of the Adirondacks, 1989).

Christopher W. Olney

Christopher Olney is originally from the Finger Lakes region of New York and has been living in the Catskills and working for The Catskill Center for Conservation and Development since 1998. Olney has a bachelor's degree in Biology and Environmental Studies and a master's degree in Physical Geography from the State University of New York at Buffalo. Before joining The Catskill Center, Olney worked for NYSDEC Region 3 in New Paltz as an inland fisheries technician. At The

Catskill Center he serves as the director of the Land Conservation and Natural Resources Program, helping to protect the region's open spaces through the use of conservation easements, land acquisition, public education, and partnerships with government and partner conservation organizations. He is actively engaged in issues involving the Catskill forest preserve, the New York City Watershed, and general, regional land use and natural resources. He volunteers for several other nonprofit organizations including Trout Unlimited, the Olive Natural Heritage Society, the Esopus Creek Conservancy, and the Catskill Mountain Club. Olney leads hikes and other outdoor activities for The Catskill Center and co-authors an outdoor column in two local newspapers. He and his wife Amy live in Highmount, New York.

About the Principal Photographer

Thomas F. Teich

Thomas Teich is a lifelong resident of the Catskills whose fine art photography focuses on the Catskill Mountain and Hudson River Valley regions. Teich works primarily with 8-x-10 and 11-x-14-inch view cameras. His color landscapes have been featured on the covers of national and regional magazines and books, and in award-winning calendars. His black & white landscape photographs, hand-printed by the artist in limited editions up to mural size, are featured in fine art exhibitions throughout the northeastern United States and in private and corporate collections. Teich's large-format darkroom facility and gallery are in Freehold, New York. Samples of his work may be viewed at www.ThomasTeich.com